American Hamburger

An American Girl in Nazi Germany

To the Westerly Library
I had many musical
events with my students
in the music room

Helen H. Buchholtz

American Hamburger

An American Girl in Nazi Germany

Helen H. Buchholtz

Old Mountain Press

3 4858 00297 5838

Published by:
Old Mountain Press, Inc.
2542 S. Edgewater Dr.
Fayetteville, NC 28303

www.oldmp.com

ISBN: 1-884778-95-X
Library of Congress Control Number: 00-193263

American Hamburger, An American Girl in Nazi Germany.

First Edition
Manufactured in the United States of America
1 2 3 4 5 6 7 8 9 10

B

Buchholtz

iv

Preface
and
Acknowledgments

To my children Heidi and Mark with love.

This book would not have been possible without the help and encouragement of friends.

My dear neighbor Norma Edgerton was the first to urge me to write down my oral tales. She began typing my tentative beginnings more than 30 years ago, as did Christine MacDonald. After continued adult education in writing at Wesleyan, University of Connecticut , and Connecticut College, being urged on by Director of Continued Education Lee Kneerim, the communication class with Gloria Axelrod brought me to the lecture podium, honed by Toastmasters International.

My mid-eastern dance friend Becky Goldstein opened the doors to the New London temples to engage me as a speaker. Schools, civic organizations and clubs of all kinds have invited me to speak. My audiences pleaded with me for the written word, both in this country and abroad. My mentors J. Anthony Lucas and Mystic Seaport Associate Curator John Gardner are still urging me on in spirit.

My husband, the former assistant to Curator Ed Stackpole of the then Marine Historical Association has edited my material.

Follow-up volumes are on the back burner.

CONTENTS

Idyllic New York Life Ends

"Ich esse meine Suppe nicht! Nein- meine Suppe ess ich nicht."

Mama recited out loud, while holding the spoon to force another round of pea puree into my mouth. I bit on the round edge of the utensil, blowing the olive mush all over my mother.

"Am siebten Tage war er tot!" she said threateningly, while I watched smugly as she cleaned me, as well as the surrounding area I had managed to spray with legume soup, up.

"I hope the day will never come when you are really hungry, and there is no food!" she lamented, wiping my face as I grinned.

"You are going to whittle down to a stick! Here, see- der Suppenkasper," she pushed the volume of "The Slovenly Peter" in front of me. I glanced at the plump lad holding the spoon in his hand. In this episode, he refused to eat day after day after day, until he finally was just a stick figure.

"Look at your thin arms!" Mama demanded, "You will soon be dead if you don't eat!"

I thought that my limbs were really not quite as skinny as his, after all. Later, when I get hungry, Uncle Hans will take me to the 86th street Horn & Hardart. I can drop nickles into the slot next to the glass windows filled with neat stacks of triangular stuffed sandwiches, or slices of fruit pie. Perhaps he will take me to Carson's Ice Cream Parlor?

"A malted a day is like a pound steak!" the proprietor would proclaim wisely, and Uncle Hans would nod and order a strawberry shake. A huge silver shaker filled to the rim with thick, pink foam would be set before me. I could refill the glass that sat in the metal holder three times. We would walk off our gained energy, strolling past the shops and restaurants, stopping to chat with Fritz, the unofficial mayor of Yorkville. Some days, we would head to the west, skirting Central Park, or to the east down to the river. If he or Papa were out of work, we would drive though the park, or around Helen's island, as they called Manhattan, stopping at the Museum or the Battery to stare at the entrance of the harbor.

"No," I thought, "there is no need to ever eat what I did not like."

Mama gave another swoosh of the washcloth across my mouth. I paged through the book of moral fables, one of the many ethnic influences which were shaping my mind, slammed it shut, and deposited it into the allotted space near Aesop's Fables, Grimm's Fairy Tales, and Mother Goose Nursery Rhymes. In a little while, I could switch on the radio and listen to "Little Orphan Annie," or wait for the shout of "Hi-ho Silver!"

Life was very good, I thought. My island was a fine place on which to live.

Mama folded my hands at night before I went to sleep.

"Lieber Gott, mach mich fromm- das ich in den Himmel komm," was the prayer that I repeated every night.

* * *

"The Harrimans are probably the wealthiest tenants," I once overheard Papa say to Uncle Hans. I was playing with a stack of flat leather boxes lined in red and green velvet, indented to hold a twenty dollar gold piece, or a silver dollar. They made fine building blocks. Of course, the coins were missing. It was after Christmas that Papa had brought them from Gracie Square down by the East River where he worked. Mama had received a huge trunk filled with clothes. She tried on an entire collection of chiffon and silk gowns that day. I was propped up with four goose-down pillows on the bed, recovering from my second mastoid operation. It brought me the first relief from pain, watching her or her reflection in the mirror. That was the start of my observing "all my guardians."

Uncle Hans had decorated the downstairs reception hall of the apartment building complex for one of the grand parties.

"Tallulah kept waltzing in; you remember how she slid across the floor," Uncle Hans said, smiling.

"Darling, she'd say!" I looked up; it was the poorest performance of Miss Bankhead I had ever seen.

Uncle Hans could never have received any kind of acting award imitating her. He lamented, "The shade of Antique White is not quite right, even though I had already matched it to the drapes."

"Yeah," Papa replied, "at times she can be a real pain in the neck! Last week, her Chow dashed passed Scotty as he held the lobby door open for her. Scotty didn't see the dog until it was out on the sidewalk."

"Bet I know what happened," Uncle Hans chuckled.

"Yeah- as manager she held me responsible," Papa said. "I ran all over Manhattan, sprinting after the animal. Finally hailed a cab. The black cabbie and I made a fantastic team. After an hour, we cornered him as he was about to pick up the scent of a fancy pink poodle at the 84th street Central Park stone wall. I pounced on the poor beast while the cabbie opened the back door. We sped back as if our lives depended on it. Tallulah was still standing on the sidewalk, berating poor Scotty. When she saw us with the dog, her eyes lit up."

"Darling, she called out. Spreading her arms she ran over and kissed me and the dog," Papa grinned. "She still thanks me every time I see her, and she gave me a generous reward."

Mama came into the room. "How about staying for supper, Hans?"

"Was giebt es zu essen?" Uncle Hans inquired.

"Kartoffeln, Rotkohl und Karbonaden," she replied. She lifted me off the living room rug, and ushered me into the bathroom. "Hände waschen, bitte!"

* * *

I loved living on my Manhattan island, in the Yorkville German section of New York City. Since Papa was night manager, and slept in the daytime, Mama would take me to the two-movie afternoon shows. Her matinee idol was Douglas Fairbanks, Jr., who also lived at Gracie Square. We often stayed for the cartoons, serials, newsreels, and the second showings. Papa would joke about our long silver screen sessions, "How were the tales of Hollywood?"

I would try to mimic Shirley Temple's dances to the tune of a record on the wind-up Victrola that I was allowed to play only after Papa had left for work.

None of Papa's friends ever really had a quiet conversation. Moderato would be the average person's conversational tone, but for them, that would only be a whisper. Papa and his friends communicated with much gesturing. They all seemed to have an overabundance of energy that needed to be blown off, like excess steam out of a kettle. I would watch them, fall into a brief shy period, and be intimidated by their exuberance. It did not take long, however, before my mother nicknamed me "American Broadcasting Company," because I would repeat all that I had heard to any and all listeners.

"Which place would you like to settle into?" Uncle Richard asked thoughtfully, looking at his wine glass filled with Riesling, addressing my father and Uncle Hans.

Papa answered, "For a working man, the United States."

Uncle Hans agreed, "You're right, Erich, for a working man. But if you have plenty of money, there are lots of nice places to live. You've both been to South America. Erich, you liked the run to Chile. How about the harbor of Rio? I remember that Mediterranean trip; stuck in Majorca for two weeks." Uncle Hans greatly enjoyed talking. He paused to pour himself some more Riesling. I sat at one end of the sofa, listening to another of the frequent discussions on the best places to live, the most beautiful spot in the world, the easiest people to get along with, and the virtues of being a good shipmate. The latter came up often, each anecdote backed up with a different nationality being preferred by the three ex-merchant seamen. I loved to hear their many yarns, and since I was the first child born into the circle of sailors that had jumped ship, they, my mother, and the other wives united in showing and explaining my immediate world to me.

Up to the age of four, I spoke only German. We shopped on the main street of Yorkville's 86th street, the broad thoroughfare that runs from Central Park to Carl Schurz Park. Restaurants ranged from notably casual to the relatively formal. Retail shops featuring sausages, smoked meats, almond paste (marzipan), and baked specialties of central Europe were situated on Second and Third Avenues. "Hab ein stück Wurst," the butcher would say, handing me a piece of sausage. "Hier ist ein Kekse für dich," the lady in the bakery shop would say, offering a cooky. The Café Geiger, Miehlke, Café Hindenburg, Heidelberg, Kleine Konditorei; ask any German- American where they went for sausage, Ehmers wurst, or Schaller & Weber meat products in New York City. They came from neighboring states as well as locally to buy the specialty items they had learned to enjoy.

Carl Schurz Park, hugging the East River, was a favorite strolling place for us. We would visit Central Park and the Zoo. Uncle Hans loved opera. My first trip to the Met was a matinee performance of Humperdinck's "Hänsel and Gretel." The witch was terrific, and I thought she had a German accent, making me leery of some of the elderly ladies in my neighborhood.

It took my mother and the committee of sailors four years to decide which church I should be baptized in. They finally all agreed on the Seamen's Church. "Pastor Pinkert in der Seemann's Kirche!" That was the only clergyman they had high enough regard for. During the depression, he had helped many a sailor, so he was to be the man "Helen zu taufen!" Mama bought me a red dress with a white sailor collar. Uncle Hans became my godfather. His wife, Tante Grete, who was a member of the Lira Gesangverein, sang for the service. Uncle Richard, my father's best friend, was present, as was his Jewish wife, Tante Hildegard, an immigrant from Prussia. She became my godmother, and I was given her name for my middle name. We drove to the church which was located on 32nd street in our Buick with the rumbleseat. Tante Grete sang like an angel. The service was quite formal. When Pastor Pinkert sprinkled water on my head and dress, I started to cry, "You better tell my mother about this. I'm wearing a new dress. Look what you did to it!" He just continued on, "I baptize you in the name of the Father, the Son, and the Holy Ghost."

I received a large certificate decorated with scores of angels, a huge gold seal in one corner, and the names of my parents and godparents. "Helen Hildegard" was printed in fancy script. It was a most impressive document, reminiscent of a tiny corner sketch of the heavenly scene in the Sistine Chapel. Tante Hildegard presented me with a heart shaped gold locket. "Well, that is your entry into the kingdom of God." She was a very jolly person, with a great amount of enthusiasm. Costume jewelry was her passion. Mama, she, and I would spend most of our total browsing time at the jewelry counters of department stores or the Five and Dimes. "Schunkelchen!" she would call the baubles, bangles and beads.

Soon after my reception into the Lutheran Church, we moved to Amsterdam Avenue. A Turk and a Lebanese family lived next door to our apartment. They had various degrees of accents. As I started to learn to speak English, I also began to notice the speech patterns of my family and the neighbors more and more. I was allowed to go outdoors after thorough indoctrination, which included, "Never eat anything handed to you by strangers. Don't go with anyone; that includes car rides, too. Never leave the block. Don't cross the street!" Other than those admonitions, I was free to roam.

Sven Johnson lived in the same apartment house. His father also was a former sailor. Sven had decided he was going to run off to sea, except that he was too timid to go alone.

"Would you like to go to sea with me?" was the earliest proposition I can remember. I asked him how much money he had to run away with.

"Twelve cents," was his reply.

"It costs a nickel per person to go by subway one way, either to the Bronx or Brooklyn. Twelve cents is not enough. We have to have some more money."

"I'll save my ice cream and movie money," he said. "You do the same."

Now I had to give up my three-scooped ice cream cones from Woolworth's, no more Jean Harlow or Shirley Temple movies. A group of sailors passed by our apartment house door.

"Wait," I shouted, "how much money do we need to run away to sea?" I grabbed one of the sailor's hands, held fast as he was taking long strides heading to the end of the block. He spoke in a foreign language, and evidently did not understand one word of what I had said. At the curb I hesitated, for I was not permitted to cross the street. I loosened my grip, and a quarter was thrust into my palm. Dumbfounded, I ran to show Sven.

"Who gave it to you? You think you can get more quarters?"

"I don't know. You will have to try, too."

A week later, we set the date for our departure to sea. We had $3.57 between the two of us. That had been the only really organized part of our scheme. I did insist on wearing a sweater even though it was 80 degrees outside. Sven started walking east.

"You will not get to the piers this way," I said.

"How do you know it's not right? Have you been to the piers before?" he asked.

"Sure I have, lots of times. Uncle Hans took me. He can tell directions by the stars."

"Well, the stars are not there now. This is a short cut."

Sven was persistent. It did not matter to me, as I had decided I was just going to see him off at the edge of the dock. I would chance crossing a street, but why should I go too far from my own neighborhood? Papa had promised to take me to Far Rockaway, and on the way home we would stop off at Coney Island.

"We are in Central Park, Sven. No ocean liners here."

It was getting quite hot by this time, so we decided to spend some of our money on a cold drink from the hot dog vender. Then we ventured further into the park. We came to the pond, hid our shoes, socks, and my sweater under some bushes, and started wading along the edge of the water.

"Get away from there," a man shouted, "you will drown!"

Sven started to run back to where we had come from. In order to keep up with him, I left my belongings under the bush. As we approached our apartment house, I saw that a crowd had gathered. A policeman was holding up a photo of me, speaking with my distraught mother. The neighbors pointed towards us.

"There they are!"

Sven's father gave him a thorough thrashing . Sven never mentioned running off to sea again. Luckily, I escaped with only a severe reprimand.

* * *

Uncle Richard and Tante Hildegard were very serious when they visited us this time. I sat on the edge of the living room sofa listening to the conversation. Tante Hildegard talked excitedly to Mama and Papa.

"Richard cannot find a job. The depression is worse than ever. We will return to Königsberg. My father has a business there, and he can use Richard's help."

"Seit ihr verrückt geworden?" (Have you gone crazy?) Papa retorted. "All of us are here because we did not want to live in Germany. Hilde, that Hitler is a dictator. Who knows what his plans are! Stay here- the depression can't go on forever."

Tante Hildegard shook her head, "Remember that fellow Hermann who jumped ship with Richard? He hanged himself in Central Park yesterday. No job, not even to ship out again. Pastor Pinkert's collection of bakery goods was all the food he had been living on."

Within the month, we said goodbye to them at the pier, waving until the tug boat nudged the ship out to the middle of the river. We drove to the Battery near the Aquarium, and watched until the steamer disappeared from view.

* * *

Besides our Buick, Papa also enjoyed driving his cocoa brown motorcycle with bullet-shaped side car. Mama and Papa both wore leather jackets. Mama wore a floppy brimmed suede hat, Papa a Lindbergh style brown leather cap with aviator goggles. On my birthday, I received the identical Lindbergh headgear in my size. We took long weekend trips into Connecticut along the Merritt Parkway in either the Buick or the motorcycle with the "rocketship," as I called it. On Papa's vacation, we drove   to Washington, DC. On the steps of the Capitol, an American Indian paused to speak with me. He was in full tribal garb, and I was much impressed with his magnificent feather headgear. He put his hand on my head, looked at me with sad eyes, saying only, "This is your land now." Papa tried to take his picture, but he had disappeared into the building before Papa got the camera ready.

After Washington, we cycled into Virginia. We even went on the Skyline Drive, to the amazement of the local cabin owners where we stayed overnight.

The weekend outings sparked an interest in my parents to move to the suburbs. Papa started to send away for Strout catalogs. Our weekends were now treks to see real estate brokers and agents. Danbury, Connecticut was under consideration, but a large mansion on Long Island that had seen better days now became the topic of table discussion. This magnificent, grand house was on Old Country Road in Hicksville, opposite Roosevelt Airport, and surrounded by potato fields. A large garden that at one time had been well cared for was part of the estate. A huge barn was situated on one end of the property, at the other end, a caretaker's cottage. The main house had a wing added to it in a makeshift manner. The owner, like the mansion, had seen better days. My father called him "Rheinhold." I never knew if Rheinhold was a new acquaintance or an old shipmate.

"Stay in the city!" Uncle Hans, as well as the other former merchant seamen admonished, to no avail.

We moved to Rheinhold's place in a caravan of our motorcycle and sidecar, our Buick driven by Uncle Hans, and a moving van. We were allotted the first floor of the mansion as our apartment. The large parquet covered living room had an upright white piano which Rheinhold said we could play. He took me into the barn, which was filled with beautiful pieces of furniture and all kinds of household utensils and toys. He pulled out a luxurious toy pedal car and a Shirley Temple doll.

"You will need the car to get around the grounds."

"Is that for me?" I exclaimed in disbelief, overwhelmed by his generosity. We later learned from neighbors that the mansion was really owned by a doctor who had performed abortions illegally. He and his family had lived there for several years, and then fled to Canada after the authorities had closed down his practice.

The replica Bentley pedal car became my greatest source of amusement. I pedaled my car to visit Rheinhold, stopping to pick dandelions for him, which he made into wine. Some of the grapes from our arbor were also used for conversion to a liquid diet for him.

My sister Erika came into the world at this time, when I was six years old. I was permitted to come into the bedroom right after the birth. The doctor asked, "What do you think of her?"

"Oh, Mama, she's all red and has dark hair, just like an Indian!"

After a day or so, she turned pink and her hair started to lighten, a great disappointment to me.

Uncle Hans and Tante Grete picked me up for a visit to the city. The big treat for me was at the Horn & Hardart Automat. The snow white cotton bread with pale green lettuce and tuna fish was my addiction. Mama called it "junk food," for she was a firm believer in the virtues of whole grain bread.

After two weeks, I was left off at Gracie Square, the beautiful apartment complex where Papa worked. It was right across the street from the New York City Mayor's mansion, and could also be reached by boat from the East River. Papa had mentioned that Douglas Fairbanks, Jr. and his mother lived there, as well as the statesman Aviril Harriman. I waited patiently, looking at magazines and at the New York Daily News until my father could take me home. Immigrants always read the News or the Mirror, for the pictorial format made these newspapers an ideal tool for expanding their English vocabularies. I was to start school soon, and was most anxious to learn how to read. The Daily News helped me, too, except that the cover articles were too often horror stories.

"You see this poor girl? She went with a stranger and was murdered," Mama would gravely pronounce.

I still remember certain famous disastrous events by recalling the vivid photographs in the Daily News.

After a few months of living in the mansion, my parents made plans to grow their own vegetables. I was given a German Shepherd dog and a tiger cat. Rheinhold rented us the caretaker's cottage, which was surrounded by grape arbors, and current, gooseberry and raspberry bushes. Mama was busy caring for 600 chickens that had arrived from Sears and Roebuck, but we had little benefit from this venture as foxes, cold, and disease eliminated most of them. The garden was much more successful, and we were able to pickle and can much of our harvest.

Papa commuted to work in New York City by car at first, then unhitched Mama's and my chocolate bullet, the sidecar attached to the motorcycle. It took the combined strength of my mother and me to hold our dog Queenie from following Papa as he varoomed off to work. He cut a classic figure draped over the big machine, his shirt tails flapping, head covered by his Lindbergh aviator cap. His one good eye (he had lost one eye in a childhood accident) was protected by a set of goggles.

Rheinhold's drinking was becoming a serious problem, and my parents decided to buy a piece of property in Bethpage and have a house of our own built. We moved in before it was finished, so that Papa could save some of the expenses by doing the interior trim work himself. Even after coming home exhausted from his second shift job in the city, he would begin hanging doors or installing electric lines and outlets. He worked constantly with little sleep, driven by his desire to provide a comfortable life for his family in as short a time as humanly possible. Mama had the new arrival to tend, as well as the few surviving chickens which had made the move with us.

"Hold the dog! Papa is off to work!" Mama would yell. "Eric, did you take your supper? Be sure to wear your woolen socks so the wind won't give you a touch of rheumatism."

His incredibly busy work load was making him more and more irritable. Weekend recreation, such as our usual little trips to the City, or even just yarnspinning sessions were now a thing of the past.

"Want to go blueberry picking to our favorite spot by the Indian cemetery?" I asked Mama one day after Papa had roared off on his motorcycle. "We can take the carriage almost all of the way up to it. The path through the woods is wide enough."

"No, go by yourself. Take along a basket."

It was about a twenty minute walk, just five minutes down the block from Evergreen Avenue, past the roughly laid out building lots to the edge of the forest. Mr. Schulz lived across the street, a hedge hiding most of his house. It was a dirt road, and the woods lined the main country thoroughfare into Bethpage for several hundred feet. The way to the blueberry patch was into the wooded area along a crooked path. I had discovered it, telling only Mama about my find. Since we liked blueberries so much, I thought that if I told others, there would be few berries left. However, I later did brag about my discovery to my schoolmates. They could not have cared less, though, for the walk through the woods was too far for most of them to venture.

"I bet you there are snakes around there," my schoolfriend Elsie said. I had never thought of snakes- spiders and other creeping insects, yes, but perhaps she was right. I had better watch out for snakes. In the way of the blueberry patch was a large clearing with several giant boulders lining it's edge along the east side. The vegetation and ground were different at this point. I would take along either a sketch pad or something to read. The time I had discovered the patch, I happened to have had my social studies book on Indians along. Looking over the clearing, I had felt a strange sensation. Somehow, I knew that it was a burial ground. Small mounds of stones had been carefully placed. It was all overgrown with underbrush, but upon careful inspection, the evidence of stone assembly by human hands was to be seen. I had found several arrow heads and flat stones which were perhaps used as weapons or tools of some sort. I reflected on how more difficult survival must have been for the Indians living in this area than for my family. Yet, Papa was lucky to have a job. Our vegetable garden, which we had started on Old Country Road across the street from Ochakowsky's large potato farm supplied us with lots of fresh produce. The blueberries we had picked would now help us last through part of the season, along with the fruits we had preserved from Rheinhold's land. As I had picked them, I had wondered if some of the Indian children had also eaten the berries from those very same bushes. "Well, at least I don't have to use the arrowheads for hunting meat."

We had been dining on some of the chickens remaining from our original stock at Rheinhold's place. Mama had refused to butcher them in the beginning. Papa had only been thinking of the many eggs we would have to sell at the stand at the edge of the property. "Fresh Eggs and Produce," the makeshift sign read, hung up only on weekends when the traffic would warrant it.

The first killing of a chicken was an awful spectacle. Actually, it was a double slaughter.

Mama said, "Eric, wouldn't it be great to have a nice chicken dinner?" That, however was not a broad enough hint, and Papa made no move to perform the needed task. "Then you also have to take care of the fat rabbit in the hutch, which is getting too small for him."

It took all three of us to catch the chicken Mama wanted for that evening's meal. Papa then swung the chicken around by its legs, trying to render it unconscious. He had then taken the bird to a tree stump and placed the chicken's head on it. Grabbing an axe, he aimed his swing at the chicken's neck, but turned his own head to avoid looking at the bird's eyes. Of course, he missed his target, only producing a gash at the back of its neck. The chicken wildly pecked at his hand, and startled, he released it. The wild, frantic cackling set off the rest of the chickens in the fenced-in yard, while the maimed bird fluttered furiously, blood dripping. Mama and I ran after it. Poor Papa was white faced, half in shock himself. Mama then took the axe and ended the chicken's suffering. She then took it into the kitchen and started plucking the feathers. I stayed by the back door watching Papa, not saying a word. He had gone into his cellar workshop, coming out with a long, slender knife. He headed for the rabbit hutch. This time, the rabbit tried to scratch Papa's hand with its hind legs as he held the bunny by its ears. He lifted the knife. I turned from the door and ran past Mama in the kitchen, and into my room.

* * *

It was two weeks before Halloween. I had been thinking of the party we were going to have in school. Our Teacher had said that we could wear costumes. Mama was going to bake some cupcakes for the P.T.A..

"We have to make an outfit for me for the party, Mama."

She did not listen, for her concern was for Papa. He had not been sleeping when he arrived home from his job at Gracie Square. Nailing up moldings, measuring door frames to miter the woodwork and hang the doors, and on and on. Maybe he would rest later, but he rarely did. He usually worked on, up until the time he had to leave for his job.

The yellow school bus dropped me off in front of my nearby friend Alloise's house. Since our new home was not landscaped like Rheinhold's property, and I had become very fond of picking flowers there, I stopped to pick an autumn aster on Alloise's property. I glanced down the road to our house, for I had been told only to pick wild flowers on land that did not belong to other people. I saw an ambulance in front of our place. Dropping the flower, I raced home. Mama's face was tear stained. I was ushered into the kitchen by neighbors. Passing through the hall, I could see Papa sitting in his living room chair, which he hardly ever used, being examined by a doctor. It seemed as if hours passed as I sat in the kitchen. Elsie's mother turned on the radio for me. Little Orphan Annie was just giving a coded message!

"Get your decoders out." I did. The mysterious message was: "Always drink Ovaltine."

Papa was escorted to the ambulance, and driven to a hospital.

The weekend before Halloween, Uncle Hans and Tante Grete drove out from Manhattan. She came with a surprise present for me.

"How did you know that I didn't have a costume for the Halloween party? Look Mama, a Dutch girl outfit."

Mama was busy watching Erika crawl around the room. Tante Grete had brought a stuffed dog for her. After eating a noon meal, we all got into Uncle Hans' car to visit Papa in the hospital.

"I'll drive you to the entrance and give you an hour, Martha."

Mama nodded. It was quite a distance from Bethpage to the hospital. I had been told that Papa had a nervous breakdown. At a park-like complex with many different brick buildings, she was left off. Erika started to cry.

"Mama will be back in a little while. You stay with Helen. Uncle Hans and Tante Grete are going to take you for a drive."

My mother disappeared into one of the large entryways. Uncle Hans drove past blocks of buildings with iron bars across the windows.

"Let's go get some ice cream, Hans," Tante Grete suggested.

I tried to read the lettering on the facade. "State Mental Hospital" was all that I could make out.

"When is Papa coming home?" I asked.

"We don't know," Uncle Hans replied.

For several months thereafter, neighbors, or Tante Amanda, her sister Anni, and their husbands drove us to the hospital. Uncle Hans and Tante Grete did not come back for quite a while.

"Mama, if you would learn how to drive, we could take our Buick to see Papa. When I grow up, I'm going to drive a car."

"Yes, you do that, Helen."

Mama went into the bathroom. She left the door open, and I heard her opening the medicine chest. She had been taking an unusual amount of aspirins lately. It seemed that every week she bought another hundred tablet bottle at the drug store when either Elsie's mother or some other neighbor took us to shop.

I had worn my new costume to the Halloween party.

"Can I go out for Trick or Treat? All the kids are going, Mama."

"Nein, das ist eine Bettelei," she answered. (No, that's beggarly.)

"Come on, Mama, you have treats for the kids when they come to our door! Why can't I go with Elsie?"

"Nein, du bleibst zu Hause!" (No, you are staying home!)

I started to carry on, and answered her only in English. She was speaking more and more in German to me, and I kept answering her in English.

On returning home from school a few days later, a shiny, official looking limousine was standing in the driveway. Two men wearing dark suits were sitting in the living room talking to my mother.

"So this is your other daughter? Remember, she is an American citizen as well. You and the children may stay here on welfare until your husband has all his legal papers in order to return to the United States."

My mother gasped at the mention of welfare.

"It should only take a few weeks, a mere technicality. Stay here with the girls until he returns from Germany."

They said much more, but I had become numb with fright. So that was it! They had discovered that my father had jumped ship! He would be sent back to Germany to go through legal immigration procedures. My mind is a complete blank as to what was discussed further that fateful day. All I recall saying was, "I don't want to go, Mama."

She was not listening. She sat motionless, staring out the window.

The dog catcher came for Queenie and Mooschie, our cat.

"I will try to find a home for them, Ma'am. The dog is a thoroughbred, and somebody is sure to want her."

We ate almost all the rest of the chickens, except for "Big Red," the most brazen rooster, and "Tiny," the dwarf chicken, who was another favorite pet.

"You can take your Shirley Temple doll and the Big Little Books, also the hardcovers. The soft covered ones will have to go to Elsie, or whomever else you want to give them to."

"My pedal car from Rheinhold, and the doll house Uncle Hans built for me are coming along, right?"

"No, you will have to decide who will hold those for you."

"Can I at least take the tiny furniture and little lamps he made for the house? They won't take up much room," I pleaded.

"You can ask Uncle Hans if he can store the doll house for you."

"Where is Uncle Hans? He hasn't been here in a long time."

"We will stay with them until we board the S.S. Roosevelt, the ship which will take us to Europe. You will then be able to see the great Atlantic Ocean, perhaps a glimpse of Ireland, the white cliffs of Dover, LeHavre, then past Cuxhaven, and finally Hamburg."

The chance to go to sea cheered us somewhat, while I made plans as to who was to receive my toys.

* * *

"Don't let anyone into the apartment. Better yet, put the chain across the door when there is a ring of the bell. Press the buzzer to open the lobby door. Whoever comes, just say your mother will be back in a few minutes. I'll be back as soon as I can, Helen. You know what to eat in case it gets late. Keep a watchful eye on Erika."

Mama was off, either to see my father, make additional selling arrangements for the house and furniture, or last minute attempts to prevent Papa from being deported.

My mother and Tante Amanda had worked together in Dr. Pilski's Women's Clinic in Hamburg-Altona. They had become close friends. Amanda had two sisters who had emigrated to the United States, and when they had sent for Amanda, she had asked Mama if she would like to come along, too.

"Amanda hat für mich gebürgt," (Amanda sponsored me) was one of the catch phrases I often heard in our family. Amanda was also responsible for securing a position for my mother as governess to Jimmy Roseman, son of the speech writer for President Roosevelt. She was relying on the Rosemans help to get the necessary paper work completed in this country, so my father would not have to leave, only to return under quota. I knew that Papa did not want to go to Germany, for I had asked him the last time Mama took me along to see him. The first time I was allowed to visit, he was sitting in a large bathtub with a lid snapped all around him.

"To sooth his nerves," the nurse said.

22

Just a few weeks later, he had been up and about, playing cards with some of the other patients in the recreation room. Mama had baked a cake for him, and we brought fruit and magazines. I did not say much. The place frightened me. Nurses and orderlies escorted us from the entrance through various hallways and doors, opening and closing each lock with a different key. Finally, we had seen my father, and I did not know what to say. Mama and Papa spoke quietly while I watched other patients. Some were playing Monopoly, cards, or reading, others just sat staring into space. One man was standing in a corner, talking to the wall.

Papa turned to me and asked, "Wie geht's dir?"

"O.K.," I mumbled, then mustered up the courage to say, "I don't want to go to Germany!"

He replied, "Ich auch nicht." (Nor I)

"But Papa, if Mr. Roseman writes speeches for the President, can't he talk to him? They have special laws that can be passed. My teacher told me that in school. Everybody is equal in this country, and your case should be heard."

My father sighed, then pointed to the man standing in the corner muttering, "I have just as much chance of being listened to as that man has with the wall."

The Great Sea Voyage

Reluctantly, I walked across the gangplank of the S.S. Roosevelt clutching my Shirley Temple doll and my school lunch box crammed with Big Little books of Smilin' Jack, The Lone Ranger, and Tarzan. In my coat pocket were the Little Orphan Annie decoding ring and a pencil sharpener in the shape of the Statue of Liberty. My father was being ushered ahead of me by two immigration men. Mama followed, carrying Erika in her arms. Gingerly, she set foot on the ship. I glance back, noticed the New York skyline, took a deep breath, and fought to hold back the tears.

"I am going to sea!" I said to myself.

The blasting sound of the steam vessel's horn announcing our departure vibrated throughout the hull. Minutes after the two immigration officers had gone ashore and stood watching us from the pier, the clang of the gangplank being withdrawn sounded. I stood forlorn at the railing. Mama had taken Erika into the cabin and given instructions to the porter as to which trunks and suitcases would go into the hold, and which luggage to place into our quarters. Papa stood with arms folded across his chest, pretending to be calm. Silently, we watched the magnificent man-made stalagmites grown out of the granite of Manhattan Island pass across our view. A brief look up at the New Jersey Palisades, while the ship's screw churned up a long, foamy white trail. Like a grand Lady aware of a ceremonial event, the steamer was escorted down the river towards the Sandy Hook Light Ship.

Mama joined us, having put Erika in care of the Stewardess. Papa had started to smoke cigarettes from the moment he had heard the ship's engines, and was now well into the pack. Mama put her hand on his arm; absorbed, they talked quietly to each other. Alone and seemingly ignored, I watched them gaze at the harbor. Mama pointed to Ellis Island. I knew what she was saying without hearing the words, for I had heard the story of her arrival many times before. She had dared to leave the Pilski Women's Clinic in Hamburg-Altona to emigrate to America, and with a position assured, could arrive like a first class passenger at the New York piers, and not be required to undergo the ordeals of immigration inspection.

Now Bedloe's Island was in full view; overlooking the channel was the most symbolic statue ever built. I put my hand in my coat pocket, pulled out my miniature Statue of Liberty while admiring the full-sized one from the deck of the ship, her right arm proudly holding the torch, reaching to heaven. How beautiful she was!

"The face is fourteen feet long," Mama called, loud enough for me to hear. "President Grover Cleveland dedicated the monument in 1886- a gift from France. Remember our trip to the observation platform in the crown, which has 25 windows, and can hold 30 people enjoying the view?"

Silently, I gazed at the magnificent, green-robed, tall lady, and squeezed the pencil sharpener until my hand was numb.

Mama and Papa hung onto each other, and then I heard them both quietly sobbing. They turned from me so that I would not see their tears. Slowly, they walked to the cabin, supporting each other. Papa needs some rest, was the message my mother mumbled. I watched the Pilot leave the ship, and stayed on deck until the last tip of the New York skyline sank into the sea.

"When will we return?" I asked aloud.

The sound of the ship and the sea was the only response. I scrambled into the interior of the ocean liner.

* * *

"The New Colossus is a poem by Emma Lazarus," Gladys, the lady sitting next to me at the dinner table whispered to me. I was still holding the miniature pencil sharpener statue, carefully folding it into my hankie for my mother to keep in her gigantic handbag.

"I'll take Helen to the library," Gladys said to my mother. Once we were there, she began to softly read: "Not like the brazen giant of Greek fame, with conquering limbs astride form land to land; here at our seawashed, sunset gates shall stand a mighty woman with a torch, whose flame is the imprisoned lightning, and her name Mother of Exiles. From her beacon-hand glows worldwide welcome; her mild eyes command the air-bridged harbor that twin cities frame. 'Keep ancient lands, your storied pomp!' cries she with silent lips. 'Give me your tired, your poor, your huddled masses yearning to breath free, the wretched refuse of your teeming shore. Send these, the homeless, tempest-tost to me, I lift my lamp beside the golden door!' "

Her words touched me deeply, for I knew how important its symbolism was for my parents.

Mama, an efficient housewife who held our lives together employing her many skills of home management and most delicious meal preparation, now used her nurse's training to help my father overcome his illness, a nervous breakdown from overwork, as well as his feelings of guilt due to his illegal status in America. The first of the two bold deeds in my mother's life was the defiant act of daring to have her waist-long hair cut to a bob against the wishes of Dr. Pilski and the head nurse at the Hamburg Clinic. The second, the decision to emigrate to the United States. Mama had met Papa through her friend Amanda, who was engaged to Klaus, a merchant seaman. My father, born in Kiel, had been fascinated with America ever since his own father had left for the USA when Papa was only six years old, never to be heard from again. Papa's brother Hans and he secretly hoped to find my grandfather in their travels, but never succeeded.

I sat crouched in the lee of the deckhouse, enjoying the solitude, and breathing the fresh ocean air. The S.S. Roosevelt, a 13,869 ton, 535 foot long popular cabin liner in regular co-service with the President Harding, the Manhattan, and the Washington, sailed to and from Ireland, England, France, and Germany. As this was my first sea voyage, I thought her to be the most beautiful ship in the world. The stack had the colors of the United States flag. I squinted into the bright sun, admiring it. I licked my lips, tasted the salt, felt the breeze which ripped the tops of the perpetually moving ocean touch me. I could watch the sea for hours, listening to the lapping waves licking the hull. The color and shading was relative to the amount of sun or moonlight reflecting on it, and I was compelled to enjoy its changing hue and mood, a practice which has become a lifelong fixation, intoxicating me to this very day.

"The world is really one huge ocean, broken here and there by islands," Jimmy, a fellow passenger a year older than I, pedagogically mentioned during one of our shuffleboard games.

"I know that," I said to myself. My Shirley Temple curls bounced in the breeze, and I wished I could spend the rest of my life on board the vessel.

"Like the good ship Lollipop," I danced and sang to the amusement of Jimmy and the other passengers. The ocean, which was so vast and at times so deceptively calm, had a soothing effect on me, but also gently rocked my parents as they rested in their deck chairs. Jimmy speculated on the pattern the gigantic ship's screw made, as we observed the wake from the stern of the ship.

"Want to see the engine room?" The crew and officers were very tolerant of us showing up in the oddest places. My nostrils had directed me to the galley, and I became friends with the kitchen staff. I was a spoiled, finicky child, eating only what I liked. The cook let me have my pick, and I shared my bounty of fruit with Jimmy. After locating the engine room, we climbed down a ladder into the noisy, oil-smelling hold. My hands were getting greasy touching the slippery rungs. The sound of the engines was deafening, and halfway down one of the mechanics spotted Jimmy.

"Get the hell out of here!" he shouted. I scooted ahead, relieved not to have to proceed any further.

"Don't you want to be a sailor?" Jimmy asked.

"Of course," I answered. "An officer, standing at the helm, or a captain." I thought, "Better yet, an admiral, or the head of a shipping line. They don't have to go into the bowels of a ship."

The wind increased, disturbing the sea. That evening, the dining table leeboards were raised to prevent the dishes from sliding off. Mama had Erika on her lap, and both looked slightly green. Papa and I continued to eat, enjoying our carefully selected courses. Gladys, who had read the Lazarus poem, was a vegetarian, surviving on mostly salad, fruits, and nuts. She left the table earlier than most, but never became seasick. Mama had scooped up Erika, and was running towards the nearest ladies' room. By the time Papa and I reached our cabin, they were both stretched out on their bunks. Papa was amused at their Mal de Mer, and assured them that they would get used to the ship's motion. He and I went on deck. The wind pressed against our bodies with such force, that we slid along the deck like skaters, stopping just short of the rail. The sea was slate grey and ominous looking, white caps were curled at the tips of gigantic waves like teams of horses neck on neck, lifting the vessel, which lurched forward erratically at first, then slowed to a steady rhythm. I found that I could anticipate the motion, swaying with the ship. I had learned the gait of the sailor. As the wind increased even further, we decided to take refuge in our cabin.

The next morning Jimmy and I were back on deck playing shuffleboard. The sun was attempting to peek through the still grey clouds, and the winds had moderated considerably. The deck chairs were all lined up. My parents, Gladys, Jimmy's father, and the other passengers were wrapped up in wool blankets, reading, daydreaming, or just dozing.

"Tomorrow we will be in Ireland," Jimmy said, pushing the disk, then leaning on his cue. "You have been a good shipmate, Helen."

I nodded, "It has been a fun trip."

Jimmy's mother had died of cancer. He and his father were going to visit relatives in Dublin.

"How long are you going to stay in Germany?" Jimmy asked.

"I don't know," was my automatic reply.

Ireland could be seen on the horizon. After breakfast, we were just a short distance from the emerald green meadows, dotted with spotted cows. A ferry chugged alongside the ship, the ladder was lowered; Jimmy, his father, and four other passengers scrambled over the side. In a big net, the passenger's luggage was lowered onto the tiny steamer. It was bobbing at the end of a rope made fast to the Roosevelt, as if it were a baby to the ship.

I looked down from the railing into Jimmy's freckled face for the last time. We waved to each other, until finally the boat and brilliant landmass slipped into the sea, and once more the S.S. Roosevelt was my only universe. I retreated to the lee of the deckhouse, sat with my arms tucked around my legs, and gazed into the ever-changing element. The immense water thumped and thudded against the hull.

* * *

What will it be like in Germany? Papa had said that they have a madman at the helm. He had warned Uncle Richard and Tante Hidegard not to return to Prussia, because of the dangers for a Protestant with a Jewish wife. I thought back about how I had begged Uncle Hans and Tante Grete to let me stay with them instead of going to Germany. He had been delighted with the idea, however Tante Grete had given him an ultimatum: "You marry me and bring over my son Hans-Egon from my first marriage, or Helen does not stay with us."

Uncle Hans had become apprehensive that his own illegal status would be discovered. He had stayed away from our house in Bethpage, and had met us in prearranged areas when he picked us up to drive us to the hospital. When Tante Grete was not along, he would lecture me on my good fortune to have been born in the United States.

"You are the first-born American in our small family." His blue-grey eyes would become serious. "The seeds of democracy are planted in your heart, and the mantle of freedom covers your shoulders. Don't ever forget that!"

I nodded, looking at his eyes in the rearview mirror of his car.

Then he would joke: "Who knows, you may become President some day, and tell them more yarns than all of us!"

I enjoyed these memories while basking in the sun and sea breeze, and did not hear my mother call. She touched my elbow, and I started to play ball with my two year, ten month old sister until we lost the ball overboard. The white cliffs of Dover were in my memory bank, collected like so many precious jewels. The brief stop in Le Havre was an education in rigging and unloading procedures. I watched the deck hands as if I were in charge. The crew had dubbed me "The Inspector."

Once again the winds and choppy sea conditions were present, the English Channel living up to its reputation. I was reading in the ship's library.

Mama spoke to me in German: "Antworte bitte in Deutsch." (Please answer in German)

"No!" I said defiantly.

"Du verstehst doch, und sprechen kannst Du auch." (You can understand, and also speak.)

"Of course I can, but I don't want to. The Germans will have to learn to speak English!"

The Island of Helgoland was visible with its white layer of sand and red soil, topped in green. We passed Cuxhaven. I saw the dikes shielding the fertile land of North Germany's fruit belt. I marveled at the beautiful hillside community of Blankenese. The Roosevelt cruised into the Hamburg Elbe harbor that day in May of 1938 as grandly as her exit had been out of New York. Only here, the landscape was closer, and she became the important star of the channel runway. Tugboats escorted her, bands were playing. Like a water parade float, we were made fast at the Freihaven. I was enthralled with the lilliputian buildings, compared to New York, the Elb Tunnel, St. Michael's church, and the Bismarck statue visible from the banks of the river.

Nervously, my father stood at the railing, smoking. Mama adjusted her large black straw hat to put the binoculars to her glasses. She scanned the throngs of people on the pier.

"Eric, just look at the fellow on the left! He's wearing some sort of brown uniform. Do you suppose even the customs officials wear them?"

Papa shrugged his shoulders, and took the binoculars to look.

"All ashore that's going ashore!" one of the crew called out, winking at me. A band was playing in the distance. There was cheering from the pier. Papa hustled us onto the gangplank. Carefully, we stepped along until we felt solid ground under our feet. Papa swayed like a sailor, and I imitated his walk. Mama had picked up Erika, clutching her tightly.

We stepped inside the large waiting hall. Mama looked about, scanning faces.

"Opa will meet us here. I am sure he received our note of arrival."

The room was crowded with people coming and going, porters and dockmen carrying luggage, passengers greeting friends and relatives. Out of the corner of my eye, I saw a man in a brown uniform approach us.

"Oh, no," my mother exclaimed. "It's my father!"

Surprises in Hamburg.

The brown-uniformed man approached us. Mama looked uneasy, and Papa's laugh chilled my spine.

"Daughter!" was the joyous outcry of my grandfather. He bent slightly to hug my mother. I saw tears streaming down his face. After shaking hands with Papa, Erika was admired, pinched on the cheek, squeezed like a rubber doll, lifted for closer inspection, and held on his left arm. I could not make out all the words, but the sound of his voice was warm and gentle. I got a hug with his free arm, and was glad not to receive the pinches which were usually lavished upon my round cheeks.

"I have a taxi waiting!" he announced, and ushered us towards the exit of the arrival building. He motioned towards a customs inspector, clicked the heels of his black boots, and announced loudly:

"Please check these papers; we have a train to catch!"

"What about our luggage?" Mama protested. Papa came to life, saying that he would carry the suitcases we had in the cabin.

"The trunks in the hold will be shipped later," the German official volunteered.

The doors were held open, and we were the first passengers to be speedily disembarked into the waiting cab. Opa was at the side of the car, helped Mama into the back seat, deposited Erika into her arms, proffered his hand to help me to the seat next to her, and then climbed in after me. Papa stowed the suitcases into the trunk with the help of the cabbie, and rode in the front seat next to him.

Since I did not have a direct window view, my attention went to observing my grandfather's attire. I looked at the red arm band with white field and black swastika, my first up-close look at the Nazi symbol. My mother no sooner had settled into her seat, cradling Erika in her arms, when she addressed her father sternly:

"Why did you come in this mustard colored uniform?" she demanded.

I was studying Opa, as I was told to call my mother's father, and he seemed slightly amused at her question.

"Why not?" he laughed, "It seems to be the fashion here in Germany."

Mama smiled strangely, and mumbled under her breath, "I still remember your Imperial Greatcoat!"

The small car bounced along the cobblestone road. My attention was now completely drawn to the passing scenery outside the car window.

The entrance into the city of Hamburg via steamer, spectacular as it was, could not top the grandeur of the New York departure. In comparison, the panorama seemed miniature, and reminded me of Gulliver observing the Lilliputians. The harbor, which is inter-connected with a multitude of shallow canals called Flete in Hamburg, consists of a varied network of waterways, artificially constructed, and incorporated into the natural Elbe River and the Alster. The latter is a lake in the center of the city. The extent of the river's banks was far too limited to suffice for the incredible amount of commerce, travel, and ferrying. The vitality of the harbor was its exhilarating, throbbing, living, pulsating embryo. From the Freeharbor district where we had disembarked, I saw the round dome of the St. Pauli entrance to the Elbe Tunnel. On the opposite shore were the giant ship basins belonging to Blohm & Voss, Howaldt, and other ship building yards, fingered into the riverbank.

From the S.S. Roosevelt, I had admired the numerous church steeples, taller than the houses, but much more modest than the New York skyscrapers. A beautiful green spire held my particular attention, and Papa's first German words to me upon our Hamburg arrival, were the description of the important shipyards, buildings, monuments, and church steeples visible from the ship.

"That's green Michael!" he said with such enthusiasm, that I believed it to be in the same category as the Statue of Liberty. Somehow, he felt my thoughts.

"Made of copper, just like Lady Liberty. Every seaman entering Hamburg admires St. Michael's church."

As we drove on, I gazed at the park area we were passing. The ride was now smoother along an asphalt road. I saw a large stone statue of a man leaning on a gigantic sword. Opa noticed me craning my neck, and volunteered information:

"That is Bismarck!" he said in German. "Soon we will be seeing the famous entertainment district."

"Millerntor on one side, Nobistor on the other," my mother joked.

"Names of the old Hamburg city gates!"

The cab driver, who up to now had just spoken quietly with my father, turned to my mother and asked, "Are you from Hamburg?"

She leaned toward the front seat, looking into the rearview mirror. "Pinneberg is Gross Hamburg, as far as I am concerned. I was born in the Eppendorfer Hospital, and grew up in Pinneberg."

"Hummel, Hummel!" the cabbie shouted. This is the welcome call one Hamburger gives another, as I later learned.

The taxi driver became a most loquacious vessel, bubbling with enthusiasm. His language was not just the stilted High German, but was drolly laced with Plattdeutsch, the Low German dialect, which had such picturesque variations, it made me smile, in spite of my still limited German vocabulary.

"One is apt to think that certain aspects of the city to which one has become quite accustomed through daily association are without interest to all visitors but to a native Hamburger like yourself," he said with pride. "Let's look at what has changed since you left for America."

Much of the verbal barrage just rolled over me, but the wide street called "Reeperbahn" was as neon-marque lit as Broadway and 42nd Street, so I could follow reading even the unlit signs. Restaurants, open-food bars, shooting galleries, Wax Museum, theaters, and dance halls rolled by in a blur.

I read: "Trichter, Ernst Drucker, Plattdeutsche Bühne, Zillertal, Operettenhaus."

Opa laughed.

"Das ist die Reeperbahn!" I heard Papa observe. "Immer noch das Selbe." (Still the same.)

We drove down the Königstrasse.

"Königplatz!" my mother called out.

"No!" the driver corrected. "Adolf Hitler Platz!"

"Oh?" my mother questioned, looking at her father. The embarrassing silence was finally filled by a lengthy explanation to me.

We were going to visit my mother's aunt in Ottensen, until it would be time to take the evening train to Rheydt in the Rheinland. We planned to stay with her father and stepmother until Papa's papers were ready to permit reentry to the U.S.A.. The taxi wheeled past the Altonaer Museum, Altona Bahnhof and the Bismarck Bath, and turned into the Bahrenfelder Strasse. A few more twists and turns, and the car stopped. Mama took a deep breath, peered out of the car to check the house number, plopped on her straw bonnet, lifted Erika, retrieved her gigantic handbag, and stepped onto the street.

Papa had paid the driver, who wished us well, and helped carry the suitcases into the hall of a four-story apartment house. Mama had rung the bell, and we climbed the highly polished wooden stairs. A massive woman was leaning on the bannister of one of the landings. The moment she saw my mother, she ran down the stairs towards her. The wide arms covered my mother's entire body in the embrace. Then she hugged my sister, who stared in amazement at her obese form. I shook hands with her, but my mother was criticized for not having taught me how to curtsy.

"It's not the custom in New York," Mama defended herself.

Papa was introduced to her, while Uncle Ernst opened the apartment door and ushered us into the living room. The parlor was used only on holidays, Christmas, Tante Auguste's birthday, and now her niece's homecoming celebration. I scooted ahead of my elders to catch the first glimpse of a round table in front of a large overstuffed sofa, which reeked of mothballs.

Anticipating every mouthful of the delicious looking pastries and confections on view before me, I sat back in my seat. Uncle Ernst rose, poured a glass of schnaps for all the adults, and with a solemn voice he announced: "Herzlich Willkommen!"

Marking Time in Hamburg-Altona.

The train arrived in Rheydt-Odenkirchen in the middle of the night. We took a taxi from the station to Opa's house. Opa opened the front door with a gigantic old-fashioned key. Dark wooden step risers and balusters were barely illuminated by a light at the top of the staircase. A large figure dressed in a long cotton flannel gown came down the stairs. It was Mama's stepmother. She shook hands with all of us, saying, "You must be terribly tired. Let me show you to your sleeping quarters."

I fell asleep the moment my head hit the pillow.

In the morning, I was awakened by the twittering of birds. I looked out the window to see a well cared for garden, row upon row of early signs of vegetables, fruit trees of a dwarf variety, and bushes and hedges that I did not recognize. Closer to the house were several flower beds, and Opa was picking some white flowers. I just watched until Mama said, "This bowl and pitcher set is for you to wash in. Be careful, it's made of porcelain. When you are finished washing, pour the water into this pail."

I followed instructions, finished dressing, and waited until my parents and Erika were ready to join Opa and Oma at the breakfast table.

"Look at the pretty Lilies of the Valley," I said.

"What did she say?" Oma asked my mother.

"Guck, die hübschen Maiglöckchen."

Oma turned to me, "Sit down for your breakfast, Helen. From now on, you must only speak German in this house!"

We all sat down to enjoy open-faced rolls with cheese, sausage meat, and home-made jam. The grownups had coffee out of a pretty porcelain china pot. Erika and I had hot chocolate from a smaller pitcher. Opa was off to work, shaking hands with all of us before leaving. He was not wearing the uniform today.

"This afternoon I must attend a fund-raising meeting. I would like to take Martha and Helen," Oma mentioned as we cleared the table.

Papa said, "I'll look at the grounds with Erika. You go on ahead."

Mama and I helped with the dishes and bed making. Oma made preparations for the noon meal. Potatoes were peeled, a large red cabbage was chopped, and a savory roast was being basted in the oven.

At twelve o'clock we had our big meal around the dining room table. Opa came home to eat with us, and returned to his job after the mid-day meal. Oma and Mama cleared the table, while I was allowed to read until it was time to go to the afternoon coffee hour.

We took an electric trolley car which had a conductor as well as a motorman on board. Oma paid him with paper money, and he returned coins from a coin changer strapped to his belt. He rang a bell by pulling a cord to signal the motorman to stop or go. It was a very pleasant way to get to our destination.

The banquet hall of a hotel was set up with three long tables. Behind the head table, displayed against the wall, hung a large portrait of a man with a moustache , and a red flag with a large black swastika on a white field. The man's eyes were incredibly hypnotic.

"Who's the man in the picture, Mama?" I asked my mother in English.

My grandmother seemed to understand, and shouted at me, "That is the Führer!"

After I recovered sufficiently, I asked her, "What's his name?"

She looked at my mother, then at me, while turning various shades of crimson. "You mean to tell me that your parents have not informed you that the leader of our Vaterland is Adolph Hitler?"

An entourage of women had formed around my grandmother, and she was ushered to a place at the head table. Mama and I stood at the sidelines, watching , and feeling rather forlorn.

"Come," Oma beckoned to us , "sit next to me. We have room for them here, don't we? This is my husband's daughter and her girl from the United States."

Mama was whispering to Oma, who then said to some of the women standing around her, "Perhaps they will feel more comfortable at one of the side tables, after all."

Turning to one woman, she said, "Martha, this is my friend Hedwig Müller."

Frau Müller took my hand, proffered the other to my mother, and escorted us to a seat at one of the side tables. I sat down next to my mother, examining the chinaware and silver with my eyes. In one corner of the room were three tea wagons loaded with the loveliest looking cakes, which were decorated with marzipan roses and squiggles of butter cream. After noticing the tarts, I admired the silk damask wallpaper. I have always had the ability to shut out what for me were distractions, and to concentrate fully on the object of my attention.

Speakers were introduced. The language, and my lack of thorough understanding, did not permit me to follow all that was going on. As I tried to comprehend, my mother tapped me on the shoulder. Everyone was standing up with their right arms outstretched, and beginning to sing "Deutschland, Deutschland, über Alles." At first, I did not raise my own arm, but then complied with my grandmother's icy glare. As soon as she looked away, I folded my arm across my chest, the way I was used to reciting the Pledge of Allegiance to the flag of the United States. I began to relax as the German National Anthem ended, but was immediately brought back to attention as another song, "Die Fahne hoch," began. I was amazed at how the women were able to keep their arms raised throughout several further stanzas of song. Papa always claimed that the Germans have a great deal of stamina. Now I understood how they trained for it.

Finally, we sat down again. The ladies now talked about the red canisters at the head table, which, I found later, were the collection pots for the welfare fund. By this time coffee was being served, and the wagons with the beautiful cakes were headed for each table, being pushed by waitresses in black dresses with white aprons tied to perfect bows in the back.

"Schwarzwalder Kirsch Torte, Schocoladen, oder Linzer Torte?"

I pointed to the cherry filled cakes, the ones I was familiar with. Uncle Hans had taken me to taste this delicacy on our trips to the 86th street fancy coffee houses. I was given a small amount of coffee, with the balance of the cup filled with milk. As I was enjoying the savory treat, the lady sitting to my left asked, "How do you like our town?"

I said, "I came at night, and have only taken a trolley trip so far. We are not going to stay long. As soon as we can, we are going back to America."

"Oh," she said, and started talking to my mother, who gave her very much the same answer.

When the meeting was over, we took the trolley back. Oma ignored me most of the time. On later occasions, Opa tried to explain the German life style to me during trolley rides, walks to the old Burg (fortress), a farm restaurant, or a scenic riverside. I started going to school, learning to write German on a small slate board. My speaking vocabulary was becoming fair, but my reading and writing still lagged considerably. I was learning from a Fibel (Primer), phonetically pronouncing the German vowels and their Umlaute (modifications). The Principal had started me off in the first grade. The teacher, Opa, and my mother tutored me as much as I could stand, and got me to the second grade within a month.

As I returned from school one noon, Mama came walking towards me. I sensed that something was not right by the expression on her face.

"What's happened, Mama?"

"Let's go back to your school, and thank the Principal and your teachers for their efforts. We are returning to Hamburg on the afternoon train."

She did not have to tell me any more, for I knew that it had been getting more and more difficult to get along with Oma. Although Opa had shocked us with his brown uniform, we got along well with him, as he did not make a fetish of his Nazi Party affiliations. He would have preferred the trappings of the Emperor's Old Guard, which he still had in his closet.

"I was out of work for a long time after the war of '14-'18. Hitler got the economy going. I have a job again."

I understood that logic only too well, for I remembered the depression conditions in America, and how grateful the people were to President Roosevelt, who had made possible many improvements in the economy. For those who do not have a weekly paycheck, the wolf quickly appears at the door.

* * *

We arrived at Tante Auguste's Ottensen apartment after loitering in the waiting room at the Altona station for several hours, so that we could appear at a respectable hour. Her hobby and sewing room had two pullout couches, which became our temporary quarters until an apartment we found on the Kirchen Strasse in Altona became vacant. I began school "auf der Elbchausee," in the second grade. Most of my classmates had fathers that were either connected with commerce or the sea. An American girl was interesting, but no oddity, as in the provincial town where my grandparents lived. I loved the area near the Elbe, which had many stately houses, and a public rose garden. On Sundays, I often walked along the Elbchausee almost as far as Blankenese, with the river in view most of the time.

Tante Auguste's apartment was on the third floor of a four story walkup multi-family house. The front faced a small public park; to the left of the back yard were formal grounds belonging to a Catholic church. I often saw the priest in deep meditation, with the Testament held behind his back, walking to and fro down the pebble stone path. The area directly to the rear of the apartment house was used by the tenants to hang out wash, beat rugs, or as a children's playground.

Tante Auguste had made me an Indian outfit, following my rough sketches. It was produced from an old leather coat she had had no further use for. The shirt and skirt were fringed at the bottom. I had made friends with a few boys on the block, and gotten them to play cowboys and Indians with me. A picture of my father dressed in a cowboy outfit was passed around and much admired, and my social studies book on Indians was an immediate hit. Germany has numerous volumes of the writer Karl May, whom they regarded as an authority on Indian life. This author had actually never been to America, but the escapades of his characters were taken as true sagas of life in the Wild West. I, of course, had lived in the U.S., had seen the Chief of all the tribes come to

Washington, DC to debate with the Great White Father in the Capitol, the time we had visited , and the Chief had told me that the land was mine now. On a small city block in Ottensen, this carried a lot of weight. Klaus and George erected a makeshift teepee in the back yard. Our clay soap bubble pipes were stuffed with peppermint and chamomile teas, and smoked, accompanied with constant coughing fits, as a sign of peace. The ceremonial dances to the sun, moon, and the rain were carefully choreographed and rehearsed. I balked at the induction to the brotherhood of all Indians imagined by the boys, which would consist of "Princess Helen" mixing blood with the braves. They were ready to lance our skins to unite our secret bond of friendship. I felt faint every time they brought up the subject. Tempers and the volume of our voices grew, to the consternation of the neighbors. The good Father in the church garden raised his eyebrows, and, I am sure his voice, to Tante Auguste and my mother, for at the supper table I heard, "This must be the last time you will play Indians! The teepee will be removed." My Indian costume disappeared, and the neighborhood once again became peaceful.

Tante Auguste taught me some German songs and folk dances to distract me from the war-whooping Indian chants.

"Wenn hier en Pot mit Bohnen steit,
Un dor en Pot mit Brüh,
Dann lot e Brüh und Bohnen stehn,
Und tanz mit mir, Marie.
Und wenn Marie nicht tanzen will,
Dann weit ik wat ik doe,
Dann steck ik er in Hafer Sack,
Und bind ihn boben toe."

After I learned the words to this half Plattdeutsch song, I analyzed the meaning and shook my head at it. Many traditions of Germany were questioned by me. Tante Auguste was very pleased that I shook hands while greeting or departing. Coming into a room with just a "Hi" or Hello" was considered ill-mannered. She insisted on a curtsey, which was nothing more than the start of a knee bend as I shook hands with her. The boys would have to bow. I considered the slight knee bend to be an affectation. Upon greeting her, or anyone else who was a stickler for the curtsey, I would do an elaborate and exaggerated courtly bow. After a while, she was pleased that I just shook hands. I did, however, like the formality of the language with the "Sie" (thou) form of the pronoun.

Tante Auguste was my mother's aunt; her mother was my mother's grandmother. She had been raised in Prussia, and had addressed her own parents with the very formal "Herr Vater, Frau Mutter," and "thou," she informed me. She was the family's historian. Her collection of kinfolk's correspondence went back one hundred years. Mama's clan had many "Auswanderer" (emigrants). Her grandfather's brother had helped build the railroad, and was still living in California. Tante Auguste read us excerpts from the letters describing the crossing of the American continent by covered wagon. They told of hardships, fighting weather and illnesses. Trading with Indians was mentioned only in passing. Tante Auguste spoke of Buffalo Bill's visits to Hagenbeck in Hamburg.

"The Indians were a sensation," she said, and looking at Mama, she winked, "The society ladies went quite overboard for some of those braves."

The Hanseatic City's History.

The coat of arms of Hamburg consists of a symbolic silver-colored gate with three towers rising above it, mounted on a background of scarlet. On the top of the center tower is the Hanseatic cross, above each of the other two are stars. Hamburg's colors are red and white. The flag consists of the emblem of the city arms in white on the scarlet background.

The circumference of the city is about 55 kilometers, or 34 miles.

It is only natural that the importance of Hamburg as one of the world's leading seaports should be reflected by the number of visitors who make the city on the Elbe their goal. Foreigners, as well as Germans, enjoy the sights of this 1000 year old metropolis. Most of the emigrants to the United States from eastern Europe have sailed from the port of Hamburg.

The great majority of Hamburg families are connected in some way with either commerce, shipping, or shipbuilding.

Businessmen of the city have shown great practical interest in arts and letters, and many a budding talent which would have otherwise withered on the vine, owes its success to the helping hand extended by some generous patron.

Every visitor to Hamburg will derive from his or her stay the conviction that they have come to a center from which emanates strong currents of intellectual, artistic, and social life. Her enormous activity forms the accompaniment to the unending symphony of labor, of which the pulsating harbor is the central theme.

It has been found to be impossible to give an exact etymological definition of the name "Hamburg." The formerly accepted derivation of Hammaburg (castle in the forest) is no longer looked upon as correct. The word hamme is in some German dialects used to denote a projecting part of a tool.

The original settlement was situated on a ridge of slightly higher ground projecting into the low-lying marshes near the confluence of the Alster with the Elbe; it is now believed that the name originated from this circumstance. The meaning would then be: Settlement on the Ridge.

The early part of the ninth century A.D. is when the original settlement from which the modern city has sprung was founded. Her geographical position made her the natural outlet for the trade that was then developing, and naturally gravitated towards the open sea.

Emperor Charlemagne desired to possess a military stronghold in those territories which had just become subject to his sway. He hoped at the same time to make it an ecclesiastical metropolis for the work of spreading the Christian faith among the savage inhabitants of the northern countries. By protecting the merchants and traders, he would have gained useful allies.

Hamburg, from the time of her very foundation, has been intended to serve the needs and requirements of trade and traffic. Her history is, in the main, the story of how she gradually, and not without first overcoming endless obstacles, developed into one of the largest centers of trade and shipping. It has been conjectured that the locality that Charlemagne chose was possibly one where the heathen Saxons performed their religious rites, and that, by erecting a church on that site, he hoped to profit by the associations with it in the minds of the inhabitants of the neighborhood, just as the ecclesiastical rulers had consciously adapted the date of the Yule festival as that for Christmas.

Owing to its position, the settlement had a decided advantage in that it could easily be fortified, enabling it to withstand the attacks of the Slavonic hordes from the east, as well as from the Danes and Norsemen from the north.

Louis the Pious, the son of Charlemagne, made Hamburg the seat of an archbishopric in 831, and appointed St. Anagarius the first Archbishop.

The young commonwealth was not destined to enjoy a long spell of peace. Fourteen years afterwards, Norsemen attacked the settlement, demolished the fortifications, and destroyed it. The small number of survivors set to work again, and rebuilt their shattered homes. This feat they were compelled to perform over and over again in the course of the succeeding centuries. Hamburg was one of the Hanseatic League cities. In 1510, the Emperor Maximilian the First conferred on her the rank and dignity of Free and Imperial City. She was henceforth declared to be entirely independent of the surrounding principalities, subject directly to the imperial crown.

In 1529, the citizens embraced the Lutheran faith, and exerted themselves with all their strength to defend it against the Roman Catholics. The latter, however, did not resign themselves to their loss without a struggle. The Cathedral Chapter lodged a protest with the Imperial Supreme Court of Appeals, and Hamburg, in order to maintain her Protestant faith, joined the other princes and cities who had founded the League of Schmalkalden for the purpose of upholding the Lutheran religion. This involved her in the disastrous War of Schmalkalden. The Hanseatic League was no longer able to withstand the growing power of the rival commercial nations, and the famous Hamburg ale, which had formed the chief article of export, and had greatly added to the prosperity of the city, was no longer in such great demand abroad. The citizens had to develop new methods of regaining their commercial ascendancy.

In 1579, a company of English traders obtained the privilege of establishing a settlement of their own in the city. They did much to foster trade between the two countries.

In 1618, the Imperial Supreme Court finally recognized Hamburg's claim to be regarded as a Free and Imperial City which, until then, had constantly been under dispute. The City Council skillfully and successfully avoided being involved in the horrors of the Thirty Year War. Hamburg defended itself against the attempts of Christian the Fourth, King of Denmark, to secure possession of the town.

After that, the trade of Hamburg began to surpass that of Lübeck, which had always held the premier position among the Hanseatic League cities.

The commerce of Hamburg assumed more and more international proportions. In 1778, the first vessel from the newly founded United States arrived, the previous trading intercourse between Hamburg and the colonies having taken its route via England. It must be born in mind that what is in our time in history the nation of Germany, was in those years a group of independent states.

The alien rule of the French under Napoleon weighed heavily on the fortunes of the city. French Marshal Davout, who expelled thousands of her inhabitants in mid-winter, is still fresh in the minds of historians. These recurring disasters were overcome successfully, however, and new progress always set in, until fate struck a fresh blow at the city. The great fire of 1842 reduced to ashes a large part of the old city.

In the war between Prussia and Austria in 1866, Hamburg sided with the former, and consequently preserved her independence as a free city.

In 1888, she finally joined the German Customs Union, but still retained the privilege of her free harbor. In 1892, she was visited by a terrible epidemic of cholera to which thousands of her inhabitants succumbed.

Originally, the City Council or the Senate were the only sources of all the political power possessed by the Commonwealth, but in the course of time it became customary to ask representatives of the commoners, such as the chief parish officials and the heads of the city guilds, to bear their share of responsibility when important decisions had to be made. Whenever the commoners found that the City Council became overbearing, they rose in revolt. These civic disorders were occasionally rather violent, but were generally eventually settled by mutual agreement.

Great constitutional changes resulted from the chaotic conditions following WWI in 1918. The Senate and the House of Burgesses were temporarily abolished when a Workmen's and Soldier's Council came into power. In 1919, the House of Burgesses had been reelected, and adapted an emergency constitution. According to its terms, the City-State of Hamburg officially forms a constituent part of the German Empire. It is a Republic, and its sovereignty rests with the people.

The House of Burgesses consists of 160 members elected for a term of three years. Its meeting are open to the public. The Senate is presided over by the First Bürgermeister and his substitute, the Second Bürgermeister, both members of this body.

* * *

My entrance into the Hamburg school system was relatively uneventful. Foreigners, especially English speaking ones, hardly made a ripple, since English is taught from third grade public school on. In a few months, I was put into the grade I belonged in. Here the battle of my name was resumed. On the cover of each notebook that I handed in, the teacher added a fat red letter "e" to my name. Just as stubbornly, I crossed it out in black. I was repeatedly reprimanded by her for this, so I re-labeled all my books with giant letters of my last name only. That year I was thereafter referred to by my family name, preceded by a sarcastic "Fräulein."

This was really the only aggravating incident I ever had with a teacher, for otherwise, I got along very well with them. On the whole, they were extremely helpful to me. The ones who had to join the NSDAP (National Socialist German Worker's Party) in order to stay in the teaching profession avoided the politics of the day cleverly. Later, when I entered the Oberbau (Hamburg's academic high school), my teachers would deftly glorify Greek history, with its democratic states embodying the ideal form of government. Omission of current events was commonly practiced, or otherwise only the front page headlines were read without comment. All broadcast and printed news was censored by the government, and troop withdrawals were always referred to as "strategic." These points were often just emphasized by the teacher's tone of voice, and the intent was observed only by those students who were in sympathy with such subtleties.

The development of educational facilities in Hamburg has been decisively influenced by the traditional Hanseatic spirit governing the public life of the city. The city's spirit was quite evident to me. Perhaps I wanted it to be there, for it became a liberal refuge for me. I believed it to be present, even of possessing a soul of its own. It was evident when I walked to the Fish Market on Sunday mornings. Push carts laden with fruit "von dem Alten

Land" (North Germany's fruit belt), vegetables from Vierlanden, and fish brought in by the cutters of Finken-wärder. Flowers, Bratwurst, and fresh baked rolls. Oh, the bartering going on: "Frische Fisch!" - "Dat sind kene frischen, dat seg ig de mol!" The quaint Platt German dialect, at times very close to English, echoed throughout the market.

The natives are quite easy-going, with a relaxed disposition, in spite of the fact that they are so hard working. Jokes are always told about their two favorite fictional characters, Hein and Fitje. Every Sunday afternoon, these two old sailors were said to spend their time at the Landungsbrücken piers, watching the constant activity of the harbor. One Sunday Hein asked if he could bring along a friend, an old sailing ship captain. Fitje agreed that it would be alright. The captain sat with them the following Sunday.

"Just look at that steamer," he commented.

After two hours of silence, he pointed to a sailboat. "She's about to jibe!" he exclaimed.

An hour later, he commented on the sunset.

"Don't ever bring that friend of yours along again," Fitje later complained, "he talks too much."

They would have thrown me into the Elbe if I had been with them, for I never tired of commenting on the scenes as viewed from the park near the Tropen Hospital, even if there was no one in my company.

Our First Apartment, and Kristal Nacht.

apa had been working on the new ocean liner "Robert Ley."
The ship was one of many that I had the opportunity to
inspect from bow to stern. The magnificent winding staircase
to the Grand Salon and Winter Garden was truly worthy of
admiration. The liner sat like a cream colored centerpiece between
the Elbe tunnel and Landungsbrücken.

I began to discover the neighborhoods of Altona. We moved
into the apartment we had found on the Kirchen Strasse. Again, I
changed schools. I had given myself a heart to heart talk not to
ever get upset about changing schools, but to treat the event as a
great adventure. It was most important to get along with teachers,
and to find a few compatible friends. However, I found to my own
satisfaction that classes in either Germany or the United States
always had the same ratio of bright students, average, limited,
indifferent, or even undisciplined truants, regardless if in a
democracy or a dictatorship.

Fräulein Daube was now my new teacher. She was about 64
years old, strict, but fair, and well organized. She always held a
short ruler in her hand, which was ever ready for action in a rap
across a student's knuckles if one dared to open her mouth for
anything but an answer to questions asked. Her little black book
listed every student's name in alphabetical order.

48

"I do not have favorites; you are all my children. I expect the best behavior from you. If not, you will get it right here!" She came charging with her weapon, whacking it down right in front of me, looking me straight in the eye. "If I want a job done, I will call on each of you in turn to help. Your name will be checked off, and I will mark down how well you performed that task. Even if you are shy, and it happens that you may have to summon the Principal or get the Janitor, you will do so."

Saying this, she turned from me and walked to the next row, staring down at a timid little girl who was cringing in her seat.

That first day, I also was intimidated by her manner, and did not utter a sound. She gave us our assignments, telling me to buy some copy books, for she wanted the best penmanship for a composition on the four seasons, written in ink. Now that I was in third grade, I was pushed ahead with lots of additional homework. The next day, my composition book was collected. Upon returning it to me, I found that she had added an "e" to Helen in red ink. Seeing it, I crossed it out in black.

"What are you doing, Helene?"

"I'm correcting my name," I answered. "It's Helen."

She never stopped calling me Helene, but she added my middle name, too, perhaps to soften the blow, for she was not one to give an inch.

"Helene Hildegard, on your way home from school, you will check up on Hedwig. She has been truant for several days. Check with her parents. I want to know if she is ill." She was putting an entry into her little black book.

Report cards told my mother and father of my progress. Any other communications between teacher and parents were not solicited.

I left the school with my Ranzel (a briefcase with straps carried like a knapsack) on my back. I decided to go home first before dropping by to visit Hedwig's house. Our apartment had three large rooms. The toilet, with a wooden flush tank secured to the wall close to the ceiling, was located in the hall. A brass chain with a filigree tassel dangling from it hung from the tank lever. Pulling it released an impressively loud burst of water to the bowl. There was one bedroom for my parents, another for Erika and myself, and a living room/kitchen with an old-fashioned hearth on one wall. Above the hearth were hooks for pots and pans. A cupboard was built into the wall, one half of which was ventilated from the outside, so that food could be kept cool. This arrangement, of course, only did a satisfactory job when the temperature was low enough to keep the perishables from becoming spoiled. There was no electricity; light and cooking were supplied by city gas.

A round table, four chairs, a china closet, a small end table, and a couch were all the furniture we had acquired for this room. The building was several centuries old. My marbles and balls would roll to one side of the room, and any liquid listed to one side of the vessel containing it. Tante Auguste augmented the bare windows with hand made lace café curtains mounted on a heavy brass rod. Four of her flower pots found a haven on top of the two wide window sills of the family room, as we called it.

Next to the house was the church the street had been named after. It had a cemetery and the pastor's house in the rear. On either side, small parks with several benches enhanced the setting. The church, known as the Haupt Kirche, also featured a smoothly paved circular driveway in front. As with so many old churches, the tall copper clad steeple had turned green with age. Equally spaced clocks with Roman numerals faced in each direction, striking on the quarter, half, and the full hour. These grounds became my play area. The circular driveway in front of the church was excellent for roller skating. The game of whipping a top with a string tied to a stick was taught to me by the neighborhood children. I had my bag of marbles from the States, but a group of slick operators soon won them all from me.

Having the striking clocks so close by, my mother did not expect me to ever be late for supper.

An organ grinder made the church grounds part of his weekly beat, and I enjoyed his repertoire of Neapolitan folk songs and highlights from the opera "Il Trovatore."

A dark skinned old man, wearing a red fez with a black tassel came by occasionally, selling "Turkischen Honig." He always had plenty of enthusiastic customers wanting slivers of the honey from the huge block on his push cart. Pieces of waxed paper, and a wide putty knife were all the tools he needed to sell his product.

On Friday afternoons, the cry of "Crabben, frische Crabben!" was heard from another push cart vendor. These were the tiny North Sea shrimp. A charcoal pot steamed small batches of them at a time, and we would generally buy "30 Pfennig wert," a small paper bag full, which sufficed for a great snack. These vendors were always well received by everyone in the neighborhood. Rows of children would be sitting on the front stoops of the houses, the benches in the parks, and even on the curbstones in front of the church, waiting for the push carts to arrive at their accustomed hours. We devoured the morsels after squeezing the tails and pulling the heads to liberate the meat from the shell, and we would throw the refuse into the gutter. The next day, the street cleaner would moan and groan, cursing the "Crabben-mann."

"Mama, I will be back as soon as I can. The address is somewhere just around the corner. I'm supposed to check up on Hedwig. See you!" I dashed out the door, not giving her a chance to question me.

It was not very far, in a tiny little Gasse (lane), where Hedwig lived. The entry way reeked of soiled diapers and boiled cabbage. A baby was screaming. It reminded me of some of the streets Uncle Hans had taken me to when we walked through Manhattan's worst neighborhoods, near Hell's Kitchen. The only difference here consisted in there being less garbage and refuse in the entry way. I looked for the house number, and knocked on the first door after finding it. A stout woman answered, and gruffly asked what I wanted. I looked past her, into a very sparsely furnished room. Hedwig was sitting on a chair, staring vacantly into space.

"Hello," I called to her, "how do you feel?"

She did not acknowledge me. Instead, the stout woman answered for her: "None of your business!"

The door was slammed in my face.

The next day, I reported the incident to Fräuline Daube. All she said was, "So." Then she made an entry into her little black book.

"Do you all know what an Aryan is?" she asked of the class.

Nobody raised a hand.

"Well, according to the new regime of Adolph Hitler, our Motherland shall only have elements of Aryan culture."

I thought to myself, now it's the Motherland, instead of the Fatherland.

"Helene Hildegard!"

I jumped to my feat, and stood at attention.

"Come to the front of the class."

51

I usually did not mind standing before the class, but this time I was terrified to approach her desk. I noticed that she had the book "Mein Kampf" open for reference.

"This girl has all the characteristics of a true Aryan."

"No," I protested, "true American, with some German and some Lithuanian."

"Yes, that's right," she said. "We will have it verified." She then read, "North America, the population of which consists for the most part of Germanic elements, which mixed very little with inferior colored nations, displays a humanity and culture very different from that of Central and South America, in which the settlers, mainly Latin in origin, mingled their blood very freely with that of the aborigines."

I was terribly embarrassed at this point. She just kept on reading. When she finally stopped, I could hardly hold myself erect anymore. My knees had turned to jelly, and I barely made it back to my desk before collapsing into it.

Across from the Haupt Kirche was a street which joined the Kirchen Strasse at an angle. I often changed my walking route to school in order to get to know the neighborhood better. While passing one of the buildings, I noticed an old man wearing a scull cap and a long white beard peeking out of one of the leaded glass entry ways. He looked so striking, like a Rembrandt portrait, that whenever I passed that way again, I would smile and wave to him. On one occasion he was standing outside, and was ushering a group of young boys into the doorway rather hurriedly. I slowed my pace, ready to greet him, but he was quite preoccupied. The boys noticed me- one in particular gave me a faint smile of recognition.

Several days later, I heard the screaming of women and children in the middle of the night. I got up to wake my parents, but they were already up and about. Papa was getting dressed, and then went out across the street to where the cries were coming from. Men's voices could be heard, in staccato military tones, "Ruhig, loss, hinein in den Wagen!" (Quiet, go, into the vehicle!)

Papa came back, looking pale. "They took the whole school-everyone in it," he whispered to Mama.

"Where are they taking them, Papa?" I asked.

"The S.S. men said they are going to a work camp, Helen."

Sleep was impossible for the rest of that night. I later learned that this event was part of what was to become known as the infamous "Kristal Nacht" (Crystal Night).

The following day before class, I told Fräulein Taube about the incident. She looked very sad and sympathetic.

"This cannot go on," she uttered. In spite of the Aryan lecture she had given us, I came to the conclusion that she had been informing us of many of the Nazi theories in a sarcastic manner.

Hitler's swift and bloodless conquest of Austria had taken place. England's Prime Minister Chamberlain's trips to negotiate with the Führer were much in the news. In March of 1939, the German army occupied the remainder of Czechoslovakia. Next, Hitler seized Memel from Lithuania.

At the supper table, these events were lively topics of discussion, especially as Papa's family had originally come from Memel.

"Uncle Hans was born there," Papa informed us. "Helen, your grandmother speaks Lithuanian as well as German. She now lives in Kiel, on the Baltic Sea, where I was born."

"Martha, is there any mail today?" We all knew which communication he was anxious to receive.

"No, Erich, nothing from the Consulate."

"Well, the investigation of my family is still going on. My job papers are being made out using my hard to pronounce old family name, instead of the Americanized form we adapted."

Mama's eyebrows lifted, and she remarked, "One of the main reasons I left here to go to the U.S. was to get away from the terrible red tape of this country. The lure of America was the promise of freedom from overbearing bureaucracies. The constant feeling that there is a file being maintained on everyone's life is one of the most disturbing features about living in this over-regulated society."

"The girls will still be able to use our American family name. Their birth certificates can't be legally tampered with," Papa said as he got up from the supper table to read the paper. Before he buried himself behind the folds of the "Hamburger Anzeiger," he addressed me, "At any time, if you should be on your own, which hopefully will not happen for a long while, you must be extremely careful about guarding your own documents. Mama has all of our papers in the brown briefcase. Your birth certificate, baptism certificate, passport, immunization papers, etc., are all in there together with our papers. Helen, your birth certificate is your key to get back home to America. Never, never loose it!"

"Jawohl, Papa," I answered, not fully appreciating the gravity of his statement until at a later date.

Once again, our night's rest was interrupted. A Woman moaning in terrible pain awakened us. The sounds seemed to emanate from the apartment down the hall. Stumbling into the family room, I found my mother already up, busy boiling water.

"Papa is out getting the midwife. The baby will probably be born in about two hours. Don't be alarmed by the cries." She then disappeared down the hall into our neighbor's apartment. Erika came toddling, half asleep, out of the bedroom. I tucked her back into bed, and covered her up. Another loud groan made her jump out of her bed like a Jack-in-the-Box.

"Stay here until we are called. Let's not get in the way- a baby is being born."

"I want to see!" she exclaimed, and started to dash out of the room.

"You'll see in time!" I grabbed her and held on. Quietly, we then sat on the edge of the bed.

Again, an awful cry.

"The poor woman- why does it hurt so much?"

"I don't know, Erika." We stayed frozen in one position until Mama finally called us.

"Come and see the baby- it's a boy!"

Slowly, we approached the bed. The mother had cradled the baby in her arm, and he was sleeping peacefully. We were in awe of the sight.

"Look at the tiny fingers," Erika said. I nodded, and we went back to our beds.

Storm Clouds Gather.

Irmgard was the first and only girl that I ever had a fist fight with. It was a tough, nasty, clawing and scratching attack. We were at it like two alley cats. Eyeing each other carefully, watching to get in a good scratch, landing a hit here or there, and finally pulling each other's hair. Mine was quite thick, and it did not matter much if I lost a few strands, but Irmgard could not afford the loss of too many. The first two pulls only awarded us each other's barrettes. We were both about the same height and age, and at first glance we almost looked alike. She had made an insulting remark about the United States, and I had countered by calling her a "goose-stepping Nazi!", as I had seen her walking with her father, who was wearing the brown uniform of the S.A. (Sturm Abteilung, or Storm Troopers). After a while of fighting, we were both so exhausted and scratched up, that we each slunk away with the other's caps.

Entering the hall where I lived, I cried with frustration, banging loudly on the door for my mother to let me in. She was horrified at my condition, and was about to wash my wounds, when there was a knock at the door. Irmgard and her mother were standing in the hall.

Mrs. S... took the initiative: "Just look what your daughter did to mine, the poor thing!"

My mother pulled me over to the door and said, "Well, look at my daughter!"

Mrs. S... looked at me, and started to laugh. "Irmgard, you sure got your licks in, too."

I was by now quite angry with myself for having gotten into a fighting situation. My mother invited them both into the family room, and offered them a seat. As she was talking, she put a coffee pot onto the two-burner gas plate next to the hearth. In no time at all, the two women were chatting, and to watch them, one would think that they had been old friends.

Irmgard was seated on the couch, and carefully glanced at me. I had dampened a washcloth in the sink, and was dabbing the scratches on my face.

"You want a washcloth?" I asked her.

"Yes, please," she answered.

Handing her the cloth, I said, "Let's go into the bedroom. We can use the mirror to better clean up."

The two mothers paid no attention to us leaving the room. I heard my mother say, "My aunt knows how to read cards, and is quite good at it, but I have heard that laying of cards is forbidden in the new Germany."

While the two of us were tending our wounds and combing our hair, Irmgard asked me questions about America. After a brief conversation, we rejoined the adults just in time to have a cup of coffee with them. Of course, ours was laced heavily with milk.

"Martha, tomorrow you and Helen must come over to our house for coffee."

"Yes, Erna, thank you. We will."

I could not believe my ears. My mother was addressing someone by their first name immediately! This is simply not so quickly done in Germany. It often takes years, even for friends, to drop the formal "thou." Perhaps this practice is the result of the crowded living conditions in Europe, where formality permits a certain degree of privacy. The casual first name basis taken so for granted in America makes the United States a very informal society.

Apropos the subject of privacy, we had plenty of it at this point in our lives. Two old widows each had apartments on the first floor of the house we were living in. We rarely saw either of them. On our floor, the front apartment was occupied by a young couple. The husband was a sailor in the merchant service, and was at sea a great deal of the time. The young woman was the one whom my mother had earlier assisted in giving birth to a baby boy, and we saw her only occasionally.

One day, my sister began suffering from severe earaches, so my mother looked up a specialist she knew of when she had been a practical nurse before emigrating to the United States. She had known quite a few doctors and dentists, having either worked for or with them. She was also aware of their professional standing. The eye, ear, and nose specialist she chose had been the head of the Children's Hospital at that time. She knew him to be a kind, generous man, as well as being a superior physician. Erika was bundled up and brought to him. Mama was surprised at the absence of patients in his private office. On the second visit, the doctor asked why Mama was still bringing Erika to him.

"You are one of the very few still coming. Don't you know that I have lost my lifelong position at the hospital because I am Jewish? We are being pushed out and persecuted because of our religion!"

The following visit, Mama took along the addresses of two prominent Jewish businessmen she had worked for in New York. She assured the doctor that they would be in a position to assist him in establishing himself in New York, if he could only get his name on the quota list.

Mama called the office from a public phone several days later, and was informed by the nurse that the doctor had shot himself.

* * *

"The citizens of a country guide the destiny of the nation. Freedoms that persons in the United States receive from the Bill of Rights belong to all, citizens and aliens alike. But it is the faith and the beliefs of the citizens that keep the spirit of this liberty alive and let the aliens and themselves benefit from it."

This quote from the World Book Encyclopedia embodies the ideals that guided us during our stay in Hamburg-Altona. As the length of our stay grew and grew, my parents began to make interim plans. They decided to buy a four family income producing house in the Lahrmann Strasse, so that we could better sustain ourselves until Papa's quota number came up. The previous owners, Herr and Frau Brunz, had lived in the main floor apartment. They now retired to a one family country home in Poppenbüttel, a suburb of Hamburg. The apartment was too cramped for the four of us, but we could also make use of the entire basement, and had a backyard at our disposal.

Papa and Mama extended our living area to the basement, which had been used for storage and as a "Wasch-Küche" (laundry) only. They remodeled half of the downstairs into a white-walled kitchen, connected a beautiful nickel-trimmed hearth to the chimney, installed blue and white Dutch tiles along the wall, and painted a wooden table, four chairs, and an old fashioned, heavy, carved hutch with glass enclosure to match the Delft decor. Mama's green thumb produced herbs on one of the wide basement window sills, begonias and geraniums on the other. Upstairs was a small entrance hall, a living room, and two bedrooms. In back of the basement staircase my father installed an elaborate blue and white flower design china toilet with a raised flush tank, to which was attached a brass chain pull. We washed at the kitchen sink, or took sponge baths in the part of the laundry room that Papa had not claimed for his workshop.

He repaired the stone stairway leading out to the tiny backyard. I would place a folding chair in the yard to do my homework, study German, or just read. I watched him cementing, smoothing, fitting, and patching, probably the first repairs the house had seen in a hundred years. He was mixing more cement as I labored over the German sea classic "Seefahrt ist not" (Seafaring is a Necessity, or a need).

"I see that the word 'not' is not capitalized, so it could also mean 'need,' right, Papa?"

He poised with his trowel in his hand, rubbed his forehead with his arm, and thought for a minute.

" 'Not' means several things, and is used in all kinds of ways in German," he said. "Need, misery, necessity, distress, or trouble. English has a much larger vocabulary of individual words. German uses more combinations of words."

I opened the dictionary to discover the 'not' variations: im Fall der Not (if need be), es hat keine Not (there is no danger), seine liebe Not haben (to have no end of trouble), zur Not (if need be), mit knapper Not (barely, with great difficulty), Not kennt kein Gebot (necessity knows no law), Not lehrt Beten (distress makes one learn to pray). That one word in various combinations certainly had many ominous meanings. I did not know it then, but it was a look into the future of our stay in Germany. Only the present moment was without danger for us.

I kept on reading "Seefahrt ist not." The Platt Deutsch was easier to understand verbally than through reading. That was another stumbling block. My parents spoke mostly high German, but they also understood and spoke some Platt. I enjoyed reading, so in spite of my difficulties, I did not consider it a chore.

Papa had completed the repairs to the stairwell, and disappeared into the basement. Better do my homework now, I said to myself. I glanced at the upstairs French windows. At times some of the tenants would look out, wave and called a greeting.

"Wie geht's mit den Schularbeiten?" (How are you doing with your homework?) the red-headed Frau Lubinski on the first floor inquired. She had two grown daughters in the Arbeitsdienst (Work duty), and her husband was a merchant seaman.

"It's going fairly well, thank you. At least part of the time I'm getting the correct article of die, der, and das on the proper noun," I answered in German.

She worked as a saleslady in a bakery shop, and did not have much time for idle chatter. So, after the initial greeting and shake of her dust rag, her red head disappeared from the window.

Herr and Frau Becher lived above the Lubinskis. Frau Becher was a quiet, dark-haired woman. She would peek out at me from behind her lace curtains, and if she caught my eye, she would wave. Herr Becher was always in uniform, either as a conductor on a streetcar, or on his day off, when he would strut like a peacock in his brown N.S.D.A.P. uniform.

The Krögers, husband, wife, and little blond son Peter, lived in the top apartment. There was an attic, which was divided into storage areas for the tenants above the Kröger's flat. Little Peter delighted in climbing up and down the well cared for staircase. Each tenant took great pride in polishing the woodwork to their landing and apartment.

We got along well with most of our neighbors and tenants, except for Herr Becher. We had observed that he was uniform crazy.

"Hitler uses people like that," Papa would say. "Luckily, he's too small a fish to do any harm."

I hoped that Papa's assessment was correct. At a very early age I had learned that grownups as well as children do a lot of wishful thinking and hoping for the best. I did not trust or like Herr Becher, even if he would not wear those uniforms. I knew that the black S.S. uniform was the one to be feared the most, for it was the one worn by the men who had taken away the pupils and teachers from the Jewish school near the Kirchen Strasse, where we had lived before.

I had asked my father what S.S. stood for.

"Schutz Staffel, originally, I believe," he had answered.

"Schutz Engel I know means guardian angel, Papa. Staffel is an echelon. Does that means it is the protective echelon?"

"The S.S. is the elite guard, the Gestapo is the Geheime Staats Polizei, or secret police. You ask too many questions, Helen. Don't worry about things like that. We'll be going home soon anyway."

I closed my book, gathered up my dictionary and homework papers, brought them up to my room, and skipped down the stairs again to the kitchen. Erika was sitting on the couch near one of the windows, playing with the celluloid doll Mama had bought for her. Mama was standing by the stove making Bratkartoffel. The bacon and onions frying permeated the kitchen. She added the sliced , cooked potatoes to the mix.

"What are we having with the fried potatoes, Mama?" I asked.

"Herring and a green salad."

I set the table for the four of us. "Are we having dessert?" I was standing by the cupboard hutch, wondering how many more dishes we would need.

"Get some small bowls for Rote Grütze."

"What kind of red grits, rhubarb, raspberry, or strawberry?"

"It's your favorite, Helen, raspberry."

Rote Grütze and fruit soups were some of the specialties of North Germany. We could get fresh fish from the fish market, and could also buy all kinds of produce from Altenland and Vierlanden, the fruit and vegetable belts of the area. The Fischmarkt was the large market my mother would go to on Sunday mornings. The fishing vessels, as well as produce-laden barges would arrive from up and down the river. Booths would be set up from six until ten in the morning.

"No staying up late reading, Helen. Tomorrow we are going to the fish market."

Mama opened the door to the basement and called to my father, "Erich, try to pry yourself away from that work bench; supper is on the table."

Papa washed his hands at the sink in the laundry room, took a comb from the medicine cabinet on the wall, gave his hair three quick rakes, and took his place at the table.

"How do you like the book?" he asked. "The sea is still pretty important to most of the people in this area, not only for the fish we get out of it, but for the main industries connected with it, namely shipping and ship building." He stopped speaking to reach for the large bowl in the center of the table, and refilled his plate with eingelegte Bratherringe.

"Martha, these are delicious. Fresh herring cooked this way are tasty, but please don't buy too much fish. That's practically all we ate when I was a boy in Kiel. 'Kieler Sprotten' is what we used to be called."

Mama mimicked the stance of a Hitler underling, straightened her shoulders, extended her right arm, and called out, jesting, "Jawohl, mein Führer, less fish!"

Erika and I giggled. We had heard several of Hitler's long speeches on the radio. I used to imitate his shouts, "Volksgenossen, ein Reich, ein Deutschland!" (Countrymen, one Empire, one Germany!)

Erika would clap, goosestep, and shout, "Heil Hitler!"

He seemed to us to be almost a cartoon character.

We finished the main meal. Mama dished out the Rote Grütze with vanilla sauce.

"Monday I'm starting to work at the Howaldt Werke," Papa announced. "I'll take the street car to the Landungsbrücken on rainy and nasty days, and walk to the ferry stop when the weather is fair. The ferry will take me across the Elbe over to the shipyard area."

* * *

We got up early one Sunday morning to walk to the fish market. Our short street, flanked by Denner Strasse on one side, and Schaumburg Strasse on the other, was deserted. My father stayed home with Erika. Mama and I went down to the Blücher Strasse, which had several black and white enameled signs attached to the doorways or outside walls.

"That's where she is now," Mama thought out loud, pointing to one of the shingles.

I read, "Marga von Herringen, Zahnartzt."

"Her father, who was also a dentist, used to take care of my teeth. We'll go to her for checkups from now on."

We crossed the König Strasse, strolled on to the Kirchen Strasse, and passed by the green tower of the Hauptkirche and our former apartment. As we came by Irmgard's parent's Gastwirtschaft (Inn), Mama already anticipated my request.

"We'll stop by to say hello to them on our way back. It's much too early now."

The tower, with its four gold Roman numeral clocks, had just struck 7:a.m.. Now we were not the only walkers- men, women, and some children were all headed for the market place, most of them carrying empty baskets, shopping bags, nets, and aluminum one or two liter capacity milk cans. The street was descending towards the banks of the Elbe. The hawking of the vendors could be heard.

"Kirschen vom Altenland!" "Neue Kartoffeln!" "Frische Fische!" "Bratwurst!"

The panorama of the market stretched out before us. Stands with cherries, new potatoes, fresh fish, the aroma of frying bratwurst, and "Berliner," deep fried doughnuts. Push carts with assorted lettuce, bunches of carrots, beets, radishes, and parsley. Eyes and noses feasted on the delights of the market. Mama carefully checked every booth and cart before making her selections. We had gone down to the water's edge, into the Fisch Halle. A few boats were tied up to the dock. The crew wore the traditional navy pants, dark or striped shirts, and peaked caps. They spoke mostly Platt, and were easy going, with a sense of humor.

"Na, mien blonde Deern. Are you helping your mother with her purchases?"

We bought some fresh herring. Mama could prepare them in a variety of ways, so that they would stay preserved. We could eat them fresh, Bismarck style, fried, or kept marinated in a crock.

"Frische Aale, geräucherte Aale!" Mama did not care for eel, either fresh or smoked, so we paid no attention to those hawkers. My father would occasionally bring home a smoked eel, which he and I would consume.

Our shopping bags were by this time filled with produce. I carried the herrings wrapped in newspaper in my net.

"Let's go to the flower market. We need a nice bunch for the coffee table this afternoon. Tante Auguste will be coming for cake and coffee," Mama said.

We also stopped by the bakery further up towards the Kirchen Strasse. The apple squares we purchased were handed to us on a piece of cardboard with a thin sheet of tissue paper wrapped around them. Mama put them into a folded box she had brought along.

"I'll put them on top of these carrots, Helen. The whipped cream we'll have ladled into the bowl I have here, when we go by the dairy."

We continued walking, up to the apartment of Irmgard's parents above their Gastwirtschaft. Mama rang the bell.

"Kommt 'rein, Martha," Irmgard's mother said upon opening the door.

"No, we can't today. We just came from the fish market," Mama answered. "We're loaded down with produce, and just stopped by to say hello. Come over to our place for coffee and cake this afternoon."

"Irmgard is not feeling well. How about next Sunday?"

"Fine," Mama said. "What's the matter with her?"

"She just has a bad cold."

"That's a shame. Please wish her a speedy recovery."

"If she's better by next week, can we go to the matinee before the Kaffeeklatsch?" I asked.

"Yes, Helen, meet Irmgard in front of the movies around one o'clock. I'm sure she'll be in the best of health by then."

Mama picked up the bundles she had placed at her feet.

"Now onward, Helen. So long , Erna. See You next week."

I hoisted my net with the herrings, and we continued on our way home, stopping at the dairy to have the whipped cream ladled into the bowl my mother had brought along.

Tante Auguste came for coffee alone that afternoon. Uncle Ernst was "auf dem Land" (in the country), tending his garden in Halstenbeck. She had baked a "Puffer" (pound cake) and brought it along; also dresses for Erika and me, matching floral dirndls trimmed in red velvet and lace around the collars and puffed sleeves, each with its own apron. She was a wonderful seamstress.

"It does not look well. My son Walter said that he expects war to start any day now."

"My God, I hope we don't have to stay here during a war," Mama lamented.

"After coffee, I'll lay the cards," Tante Auguste promised.

Later, I helped clear the table. Papa went into his workshop. My mother locked the front door, and pulled the drapes of the living room windows closed. Tante Auguste got out a deck of cards from the folds of her gigantic handbag. She shuffled them, and had Mama cut them three times. She sat in the middle of the sofa, like a fat Buddha, with the table in front of her. My mother and I sat on either side. One by one, she lay the cards down.

Finally, she said, "It does not look well for you! Not at all!"

Cultural Differences.

räulein Daube did not only read us excerpts from "Mein Kampf," she also introduced her students to the New Testament, hoping to turn us into good Christians. Four weeks before Christmas, she brought in a pine advent wreath, suspended it from the ceiling with ribbons, lit one candle of the four every week, and taught us songs in anticipation of the holiday. "Alle Jahre Wieder," "Ihr Kinderlein Kommet," and "O, Du Fröhliche" were sung. The loveliest of Weihnacht's lieder, "Stille Nacht, Heilige Nacht" was harmonized nearest Christmas Eve. It rang out with enthusiasm and religious conviction by most of us.

The tradition of the tree had originated in Germany, and was, of course, observed in our household. In the United States, we had followed the practice of expecting Santa Claus to come in the night; presents were opened in the morning. Now we observed the German custom of "Bescherung" (distribution of gifts) on Christmas Eve, followed by two days of "Weihnachts Tage."

We had a surprise guest that Christmas Eve. Santa Claus looked very familiar to me, but I dismissed the similarity as being perhaps a neighbor look-alike, but no, it was Opa. Oma had died of a heart attack after attending one of her fund raising sessions for the Führer. Opa was very lonely, and hoped we would not turn him away.

"The uniform is in the closet, together with the Kaiser's trappings," he assured us.

It was a festive holiday, with the scent of a fresh pine tree illuminated by two dozen white wax candles, lots of beautiful ornaments, glittering tinsel, Schocoladen Kringel (chocolate rings), Lebkuchen, oranges , and red winter apples. I received a fashion doll that was subsequently always kept dressed in original creations fashioned from every scrap of material available to me. Tante Auguste had taught me how to knit and crochet, and had supplied me with leftover yarns and wool. Opa added to my book collection with Deutsche Helden Sagen (German Hero Legends). I also had the Brothers Grimm and Hans Christian Anderson fairy tales, and poetry by Goethe and Schiller. We had stuffed goose, red cabbage, baked potatoes, and berry compote for dinner. Opa wished us a merry Christmas and a Happy New Year, and expressed hope that our plans to return home would work out for us some day.

Mama and I brought him to the train station, and dropped by Tante Auguste and Uncle Ernst before returning home. We exchanged gifts with them. Tante Auguste had tailored a blue-gray Russian style coat with gray Persian lamb trim, and matching fur hat and muff for me. I thought it was the most beautiful outfit in the world.

I remember admiring her talent. "I would love to learn how to sew," I implored her.

Somehow, we never found the time for that. She did get me a song book, but I could not read music at that time, so she hummed the melodies while I learned the texts.

Upon returning home, I taught Erika some of the lieder, and we became quite proficient at harmonizing. The radio was a very dear source of entertainment for us. Wunschkonzert (a write-in music program) on Sundays could be heard coming from surrounding households, including ours. Music and dance meant much to me. My feet moved to any beat. I could simply not sit still listening to the tunes of the lovely Strauss waltzes, and operetta and opera music of Lehar, Mozart, and Verdi early became life-long favorites. By this time, the every day hit parade songs I had heard in America, such as "The Merry-Go-Round Broke Down" and "Jeepers, Creepers" were being replaced by German Schlager (hit tunes) and marching songs. The latter were part of the constant bombardment of slogans and propaganda being disseminated by the government. Some of the war songs from WW1 were dusted off, and reused against the same anticipated enemy, England.

"In England wohnt ein kleiner Mann,
Der zieht sich wie ein Mädchen an.
Er ist nicht klug, er ist nicht schlau,
Er ist nur eitel wie ein Pfau."

A derogatory stanza in which Anthony Eden or Winston Churchill were satirized was popular, but the Führer and his cronies were strictly exempt from public criticism or ridicule. All communications on radio or in newspapers were under iron control of the government. Art was prescribed. Womanhood, work, and the German people were exalted. Among the people, many jokes and humorous anecdotes nevertheless made the rounds, poking fun at Göbels' propaganda, and Göring's passion for food and opulence. The "Wochenschau," a weekly film providing current news was always shown before the main feature at theaters.

In an effort to come to grips with all of the changes coming into my life, I spent a good deal of time in serious meditation, comparing the two cultures I had been exposed to at an early age. Some things new and different were taken in stride, others were more difficult to absorb. I had difficulty in understanding the shock and verbal barrage that some of the Germans loosed on colorful dress, different manners, food or beliefs other than what they thought to be the norm. The homes of seamen or merchants were not quite as critical of an unusual costume, but others were quite provincial in their outlook.

Families with more than three children were subsidized. The kitchen was as important as it should be for the survival of individuals in the households. Women had good household skills, but also had other vocations. My family chose to go to women doctors and dentists.

* * *

Another letter from Tante Hildegard arrived, to my delight. I was so exited about it that I even failed to check for a communication from the American consulate, which we were always waiting for. I wondered how she was doing. Will she come for a visit? Or perhaps I could travel to Königsberg, and spend school vacation with them. I urged my mother to hurry and read the letter.

"Oh, Mama, wouldn't it be great to see them again? We could talk about the States, and our shopping trips to Klein's department store. Remember when Tante Hildegard found a blue floral dress on sale, and another lady also grabbed it at the same time? Neither wanted to let go, and they started a tug of war. All of a sudden she released it, and the woman fell back into a rack of dresses. Tante Hildegard said, 'It wasn't my size, anyway. Let her have it!' "

Mama opened the envelope with a long, slender blade with an ivory handle, which was kept in the living room bureau. She sat down on the sofa to read the letter. It was several pages long, and I was anxiously watching her. The first few paragraphs brought no changes to Mama's expression, but as she turned the pages, I knew that the letter did not bring good news.

She looked up, saying to me, "Helen, you remember the Jewish school across the street from us, before the S.S. took the pupils and teachers to a labor camp? They all had to wear yellow stars of David with "Jude" written on them. Tante Hildegard has to wear one, too."

"Can't she go back to New York?"

Then I remembered why she had left America in the first place. It was because Uncle Richard was unable to find work in the depressed labor market that they had returned to Prussia.

"Is Uncle Richard working now?"

"Yes, he is, but they should have never left New York. Now let's hope that she doesn't have to go to a labor camp."

My prayers, that I had started at an early age rather mechanically, now took on greater meaning.

* * *

My knowledge of geographical places, ships, museums, the German language and literature, was increasing. Fräulein Daube had summoned my mother to discuss transferring me to the middle school, since I was now to be pushed ahead one grade.

"Let her relax a little in your class, Fräulein Daube," Mama told her. "When we get moved into our house she will have to change schools again. We'll put her in the fourth grade at that time."

Signs of war now became more and more evident. Open mobilization had started, and the war broke out after a few months. We then realized that it would most likely have to be all over before we could hope to return to America. Home became a distant, utopian dream, which would only perhaps someday materialize.

68

Preparations for defense were going on in the park near our house. Zigzag trenches, "Luftschutz Gräben" (air raid ditches) were being dug. The park had been used as a mass burial ground for victims of the terrible cholera epidemic of 1892, and many skulls and bones were being unearthed in the process. Irmgard and I were playing tag with some of the neighborhood boys, jumping over mounds of earth, or hiding in the six foot deep trenches. I let out a shriek when my foot landed on one of those skulls. One of the boys picked it up by its flowing red hair, and chased me with it.

The neighborhoods were divided into districts under the jurisdiction of leaders called "Gauleiter," and we also had a "Luftschutzwart" (Air Raid Warden).

"These are only practice arrangements," he assured us, "nothing to get alarmed about. Just darken all your windows at night."

Mama bought black shades, and I began saying more lengthy prayers at night before going to sleep.

* * *

My parents read the "Hamburger Anzeiger" daily, but it contained no Sunday comics, which I dearly missed. What was happening to Dick Tracy and Smilin' Jack? Were the adventures of Little Orphan Annie still on the radio? A ring of the door bell interrupted my reminiscing. Mama went to answer the door. After a few moments, she called me into our hall. A young girl of about fourteen years of age, wearing a white blouse with black tie held together with a brown leather Turk's head knot, was standing in the front entry way. Mama did not invite her into our apartment.

"This girl would like to speak with you," Mama said.

The girl had chestnut hair, bound by a single braid which reached halfway down her back. I noticed that she was cross-eyed, and felt uncomfortable trying to decide which eye to look into. My mother stood behind me, listening to our conversation.

"Why haven't you come to Dienst (duty)?" she immediately berated me. "Don't you know that it is your obligation?"

I looked at her in wonderment, then turned to my mother. "What obligation, and to whom?"

She gave me the same look of exasperation that my grandmother in the Rhineland had given me.

69

"To the Führer, of course!" the girl clarified.

"Oh, him- what does he want of me?"

The girl became quite agitated and turned red in the face. She took a handful of papers out of a briefcase, and thrust them at me.

"Fill these out, and read all the literature. You will be questioned on them, and you are expected to be thoroughly familiar with all of the Führer's trials and tribulations." She snapped her briefcase shut, snapped herself to attention, and raised her right arm in the now all too familiar salute.

"Heil Hitler!" she shouted, turned to the front door, and disappeared down the street. Mama and I were absolutely dumbfounded at this comic opera performance, and held our hands over our mouths to stop our convulsive laughter. We took the papers into the living room to look them over. One of the slips was a personal questionnaire, another was a membership card to be filled in, with a space for a seal. The rest of the material consisted of a brief recounting of the life story of Adolph Hitler, and the political struggles of him and his Munich Putsch revolutionaries.

During one of my visits with Irmgard, I related the story of the meeting with the Hitler Youth leader.

"You'll have to go, I hope you realize," she said, looking very serious.

"Irmgard, it's great that you feel obligated to attend those sessions, but I really can't spare the time. I promised my new teacher, Fräulein Plaas, that I would study hard for the city-wide exams for entrance into the Oberbau, since I felt ill at ease with entering the Lyceum."

"Helen, don't you feel the pull of the Motherland? How could your parents ever have left such a beautiful place as Germany? Just look at this great city of Hamburg!"

We were walking by the park grounds near the Tropical Hospital, overlooking the bustling harbor. She certainly was right about the beauty of this clean, well-cared for city.

"Irmgard, you're much too nationalistic, although I do understand your love of the city. I love it, too, but I have to return to where I was born. I love the United States more."

"But your parents are German! You have to go to Dienst!"

"That's debatable, Irmgard," I said firmly.

We continued our walk over to the Bismarck monument, down the wide avenue to the Landungsbrücken. The ship "Guslaff" had taken the place of the "Robert Ley." We walked along the waterfront to the Fischmarkt, came up from the Elbe, and stopped off at her parent's Gastwirtschaft for an apple flavored soda. Her father was working at the courthouse, and the pub was being run by either her mother, or hired help. It was a wholesome, family type establishment, with a large dance hall in the rear, which was only being used to store tables and chairs at this time, as dancing was now prohibited until the end of the war. The singing of patriotic songs was, however, always encouraged. Irmgard and I used the stage as our own private gym. We practiced calisthenics, which bored me after a while, so I made up dance routines to the music of a phonograph.

"You are not supposed to dance till the war is over," Irmgard chided.

"I have to practice so I don't forget," I said, continuing my gyrations of mideastern and Indian movements that I had only read about. We would rehearse skits, and charge the neighborhood children a few pennies to watch our shows. At times, Irmgard would invite her cousin Günther, who went to the Gymnasium School, to our presentations. He had dark, wavy hair, and light blue, serious eyes. He watched me intently, making me self-conscious and nervous, and caused me to muff my lines.

"What's gotten into you? He's only my cousin. I've known him all my life." Then she stopped when she realized that I had taken an interest in him. "He's smart, though, the gifted one in the family."

Embarrassed, I told Irmgard that it was nearly time for me to meet my father, who would be walking up from the harbor, so I asked her to see me on Sunday to attend the movie matinee performance of Heinz Rühman in "Quax der Bruchpilot." He was one of our favorite comedians. The week before, we had seen him in "Der Mustergatte."

A dark blue-clad wave of shipyard workers came up the inclined street, Papa among them.

"I have tickets for you and Mama to go to the operetta on Saturday," he informed me.

Theater, operetta, opera, and variety show presentations were part of the "Kraft durch Freude" (Strength through Joy) programs every worker could take advantage of should he or she wish to. Their children were also eligible to participate in four-week summer camps.

"Helen, I made arrangements for you to take the train to Haffkrug, on the Baltic, for recreation. By the way, be sure to keep up with your English."

"I'm taking it in school now. The teacher has a marvelous British accent. He says he never heard English spoken the way I do."

"What?" exclaimed my father.

"Yes, I asked him if he had ever visited New York. His answer was that he had, as a guest of the British Embassy."

Papa laughed, "They must have kept him locked up with a bunch of limeys!"

* * *

As soon as the school term was over for the summer, I left by train with a gathering of one hundred boys and girls aged nine through thirteen for the Baltic area. We were taken to a large villa-like children's health resort directly on the Baltic shore. The girl's dormitory was a ceramic tiled room with gigantic French windows, which were kept open at night to let in the salt air and the soothing sounds of the perpetual motion of rushing waves. This was a glorious way to be lulled to sleep, and insomnia was never a problem here.

A loud gong roused me from my peaceful slumber and a voice which a boot camp drill Sargent would be proud of ordered us out of bed.

"Take turns at the twenty sinks along the back wall, gargle with sea water from this pitcher, and make up your beds without a wrinkle. Smooth out the sheets and blankets, and tuck in all the corners!"

Our bedmaking skills were then carefully checked, and those not meeting the rigid criteria of our inspector were unceremoniously pulled apart. Each of our lockers received the same treatment, clothes being yanked out onto the floor if orderliness was wanting.

We were dressed in warm-up suits, which we were required to wear most of the time. After lining up at the door, we were ushered out of the building, and ordered to jog to a wooded area in the rear of the brick home. We formed two large circles in a clearing, with the drill Sargent in the center. She led us in a series of jumping jacks, followed by various arm exercises.

"Eins, zwei, drei, vier!" her thin lips chanted. Then, as she began running again, we followed like sheep, to be finally herded to the dining room for breakfast. We held hands, called out, "Guten Appetit!" and sat down to fall over the food like hungry lions. Those of us without a weight problem were permitted second helpings. There were two quite obese girls among us whose diets were strictly controlled. Hannelore, who sat next to me, was allowed only a small dish of stewed fruit and a glass of milk. This regimen, as part of her overall diet, was successful, and she began losing two or three pounds a week.

After breakfasts, we took long walks along the beach or to the nearby forest. We would return for a noon meal of vegetables, potatoes, meat, and stewed fruit for dessert, followed by an hour and a half nap. In the afternoons, weather permitting, we could go swimming in the Baltic Sea; otherwise, we took turns rowing a fair-sized skiff.

The drill Sargent or an assistant were always with us. They would inspect our ears, throats, and nails every evening.

"What do we have here?" She embarrassed me, pulling my ear.

"I had two mastoid operations on that ear. I'm happy that I can even hear," I replied.

I got the impression that the drill instructors really enjoyed harassing us, and nit-picking several of us at every opportune moment seemed to become one of their favorite pastimes.

I was so exhausted after the first day's events that I looked forward to falling asleep immediately.

"Lights out at nine. No more talking. Good night!" came the orders from our drill Sargent.

"Hey, America, tell us about your country," a voice from the far side of the room requested.

I was wrapped up in my own thoughts, still smarting from that yank on my ear, and paid no attention to the query.

"Stuck up American, can't even answer. Or maybe you don't know how." I was being goaded into responding.

"I'll talk to you tomorrow. Good night for now."

The door was pushed open. The drill Sargent stood silhouetted in the frame. "Don't want to sleep, eh? Get your blankets and stand out in the lighted hall!"

I remember falling asleep while standing, and collapsing to the floor, only to be roused and ordered to get up and keep my eyes open. After a time judged to be sufficiently disciplinary, we were permitted to return to bed. The next morning I asked Hannelore, whose bed was on the far side of the room, if she knew who had been the smart aleck causing us to be punished.

"That's Gerda, over there."

I walked up to her and threatened, "I hear you want to know about America. Well, I was raised by Indians, and if I have to stand in the hall again because of you, I'll show you some of the ways Indians have of getting even!"

She looked at me with surprise, and I turned away quickly so that she would not see me smile. I returned to my bed to find the drill Sargent inspecting my housekeeping. Everything was tucked in properly, and I was relieved to find that I had passed inspection. Down the stairs we all flew, running through the forest as silently as Indians now.

"America," a boy's voice called out, "do you know sign language?"

"Oh, I'm in for it now. Someone's calling my bluff," I said to myself, pretending not to hear.

The boy came up to me, introducing himself. "I'm Helmut."

Raising my right hand, I answered, "I'm Helen. How!"

Friday and Saturday evenings, after supper and until bedtime, we had dances. Children were apparently exempt from the dance ban that Irmgard had told me about. Polkas, waltzes, and foxtrots were played on the phonograph, and the boys would be expected to come over to the girls seated in a row against a wall, bow, and request a dance. I took turns dancing with Helmut and Karl Heinz, who became engaged in a mild rivalry. At that age, the boys shuffled rather than danced. They were, however, not shy about talking, and they never tired quizzing me about Indians, Hollywood, and Chicago gangsters. The social contact with the boys furthered my own interest in learning more about the subjects I was assumed to be an expert in. I could bluff my way through the Indians and Hollywood, but all I really knew about gangsters was the little I had heard about Al Capone and something about a massacre on St. Valentine's Day. Now I began reading detective and spy stories during my nap time. I also took a biography of Buffalo Bill out of the camp library to bone up on Wild West lore.

We began story telling sessions, and I assumed the role of a Scheherazade.

"I was riding on the express elevator to the observation deck of the Empire State Building, when turning, I spotted Al Capone's hit man in the crowd. How did I know who he was? He looked like George Raft, flipping a silver dollar. The woman with him, the spitting image of Jean Harlow, was saying something about wanting to be alone." The more preposterous my tales became, the more the children enjoyed them.

* * *

Physically fit and tanned, I arrived at the train station in Hamburg. My parents and Erika were there to pick me up, and took me to a café on the Mönkeberg Strasse for refreshments. Hannelore was sitting at the next table with her parents. Her mother was lamenting how thin she had become.

"You'll just have to have lots of cake, so you'll look right again."

Look right! Poor Hannelore was still far too much overweight, as were her enormous parents, who even rivaled Tante Auguste in proportions.

Mama was telling me the latest of her family. Tante Auguste had two sons, who were my mother's cousins. One of them, Walther, was an engineer, and married to a girl named Klara. They had become the closest friends my parents permitted themselves to have. We would visit each other's homes, and my parents would go to the Reeperbahn, the theater, or party with them. Tante Klara often came for Kaffeeklatsch, bringing the latest news.

My mother's grandparents had settled in the small town of Pinneberg around the turn of the century, and Mama had been born there. We always referred to them by group name as "die Pinneberger." A great-aunt of my mother, Tante Paula, was one of the most colorful of these relatives. She still had a Prussian accent, and talked about her husband having fought the Russians in WW1, and bringing back two young wolves which they kept on the family farm, much to the dismay of the neighbors.

"Helen," Tante Paula would say with her eyes shining, "your grandfather never had to buy himself a drink in the pub. The patrons would pay him to do those energetic Russian dances. He was the best dancer of them all! The local musicians would accompany him while he leaped, jumped, did deep knee bends, and kicked to the rhythms of 'Dark Eyes', 'The Song of the Volga

Boatmen', and other Russian melodies. He spoke Russian, too, and sang loudly on his way home from the local tavern."

Mama also often spoke about my great-grandfather's delight in dancing and singing. I suspected having some of the Nomadic eastern blood in my veins; my high cheekbones tend to bear this out.

Tante Erna and Uncle Henry were more of "die Pinneberger." They invited me to a "Schlachtfest." The hog that they had fattened was to be butchered. The killing of the porker was to be professionally done, but my feeling was that one could very well do without witnessing that event. This down side is, however, quickly forgotten when one participates in the preparation of the numerous sizes, flavors, textures, and shapes of sausage making. These are the mainstay of the German diet; liverwurst, bloodwurst, headcheese, and knockwurst smoked and boiled in infinite variety. The country scene was a marvelous learning experience for a city girl. The tasting of these sausage products was about the last of any adequate meat supply I was to have for a very long time.

War Jitters.

After completing many of the interior improvements to our investment property, my father decided to paint the front of the building. He rented and erected scaffolding in preparation for this project. The neighborhood boys took advantage of what appeared to be a ready-made jungle gym, and were swinging like monkeys from the lower rungs. Heinz was showing off, demonstrating how many Klemzüge (chin-ups) he could do, hoping that I would be paying attention to his gymnastic abilities. Papa went to work with a vengeance, and soon the house was the cleanest and freshest looking on the block. He took inventory of the upgrades he had accomplished: he had plastered, painted, wallpapered, repaired woodwork, re-bricked and cemented the back stairs and the small backyard. In addition, he had white washed the entire basement, and laid out his workshop in the former "Waschküche." Part of the basement hallway had been sectioned off for food storage as well as potato and coal bins, and a sandbox for fire fighting had been built. The sandbox also served a dual purpose, by permitting carrots to be stored until they were dug out for our consumption.

The two wide recessed windowsills of our white-walled, blue-trimmed kitchen were displaying geraniums, begonias, and herbs. The hearth's metal was gleaming, briquets were burning, kettles and pots simmering and bubbling, producing wonderful aromas throughout our apartment. Currants, gooseberries, and raspberries were jellied and jammed. Mason jars were in readiness for the

77

anticipated vegetable harvest. Camomile, dill, mint, parsley, and woodruff were gathered and dried. Later, apples, pears, and plums would be desiccated to become additional storage supplies.

"We will not starve!" Mama cheerfully exclaimed in the midst of feverish preparations. Papa was wood-turning bowls on his lathe, and manufacturing toys and parts of wheelbarrows and carts for barter. He, too, was confident that these items would assure us a comfortable survival. His motto: "When commodities become scarce, we'll trade." Our family was busy planning to survive a war. The blueprint for my parents was their WW1 childhoods in Kiel and Pinneberg. We all fervently hoped for a speedy end to the war, whatever the outcome might be. I sought consolation through religious training at the Hauptkirche. The Pastor could not tell me the worth of human beings forced to wear a yellow Star of David, nor of the rights of dark-eyed gypsies to live in a free society. Mechanically, I learned the ten commandments like another ballad or epic poem. More and more, I would engage in daydreaming, transporting myself to places I had been to in the United States. I visualized myself on a Long Island beach, on a rocky New England coast, or in the midst of the ocean in either smooth, sunny weather, or engulfed in tempestuous, foaming seas. I had trained myself to concentrate on mentally transporting myself to a desired location to avoid the dread of being bombed upon during an air raid, to block out the aggravating radio news broadcasts, and later, to ignore the frequent pangs of hunger.

I viewed my immediate surroundings as though I were looking through a window at a stage play. I often felt like an actor in a production, but lacking the necessary skills of a player. Inasmuch as I had no peer group that I wished to identify with, books became my most important pastime. I soon realized, however, that they, too, were capable of subtle indoctrination.

The teachers I had were for the most part quite skilled in their respective domains. Geography and history lessons centered around Germany as if it were the only country that the sun shined upon, and all others doomed to perpetual darkness. I, as a misplaced American, remember asking questions in class that were daring and actually considered subversive for the times, and receiving straightforward and honest answers. My teachers were also not averse to comment, "If I only knew the answer!" Greek democracy was used to illustrate the ideal form of government, although it assuredly was not part of any curriculum for that age group. Teachers became my friends and heroes. The people I most detested were the bureaucrats. Since our apartment house was subject to certain property taxes, my mother and I would go to the Rathaus (City Hall) to either pay the taxes, or to apply for permission for whatever improvements my father planned to make to the house and his workshop. His large assortment of machines, including lathes, drill presses, circular saws, polishers, etc., occasionally caused power failures which once even affected our entire neighborhood. To avoid such problems, we applied for heavier electric service to our house. Our typical experience was to have to wait for hours in the high ceilinged anti-hall of the municipal building until the first syllables of our Lithuanian name would be incorrectly puffed out by the official in charge.

An additional ten year advance tax burden requiring a second mortgage was levied against property owners in order to pay for Hitler's military budget. Bureaucrats had accumulated huge dossiers covering the lives of families with other than ordinary backgrounds which, of course, included us. After entering the Oberbau school, my progress was carefully monitored by bureaucrats hoping for a slip in my grades, which would give them an excuse to put "the American" into the menial labor market, and free up my school slot for a German student. The faces of these self-righteous creatures all had the same constipated expression. I am not usually given to generalizations, but my later experiences working as a law apprentice, where some of my duties included visiting different municipal agencies to gather data for the firm that employed me, certainly supported my earlier impressions. I would use my anti-weapon, smiling broadly no matter how preposterous I found their behavior. A number of times a laugh could not be suppressed, and the required rubber stamp or permit was withheld because of it. I would try play-acting, and apologize in the most serious manner for my lack of comprehension of the German language, or by clicking my heels to mimic the Heil Hitler stance. The lower the status of the official, the more of a run-around we would be subject to. My mother had to threaten to go on welfare unless our American money confiscated by the bank would be paid out to us in German currency. This was in sharp contrast to her proud refusal to go on welfare in the U.S., but the dollars were promptly released.

Our numerous visits to the Hamburg as well as the Altona Rathaus and other municipal buildings stimulated my interest in the architecture of public structures. The unpleasant human contact were dismissed from my mind, and the beauty of the buildings was much admired. Systematically, I explored various sections of the city. The museums, music halls, churches, fountains, statues and parks were on my inspection tours. I always found an excuse to include the harbor, for the water drew me like a magnet. I enjoyed sniffing the brackish mist of the Elbe. I would say to myself, as I gazed out from the Landungsbrücken, or traipsed through the Elbe Tunnel, "Hamburg ist ein schönes Städtchen" (Hamburg is a pretty little city). Nothing, however, could replace the splendor of the Hudson River with the mighty green lady guarding my New York.

* * *

In years to come, the one I felt most sorry for in our family was my sister. She had been born in Oyster Bay county on Long Island, in the cottage we had been renting prior to our move to the house that we had built, and had been only a tot when we came to Germany. I realized that she knew very little about America. I tried to teach her the nursery rhymes and songs that I remembered, but most of all to tell about my 22 square mile island.

"What island are you talking about?" she would intervene, while I tried to imitate the serious demeanor of a pastor preaching a sermon. I felt so enlightened, self-confident, and positive in my belief in my own island, that Erika and the neighborhood children would stop whatever raucous cries they were emitting in our little backyard to listen. My pencil sharpener in the shape of the Statue of Liberty was held up like a crosier, or symbol of authority.

"Even with eyes closed, the odors and sounds form one section to another are distinct." I would close my eyes and continue my reminiscing , wandering mentally out of the Yorkville neighborhood to others in different parts of the city. The music from the coffee houses and restaurants towards Second Avenue, and down to the seventies, rang in my ears. Polkas and czardases of the Hungarian section, combined with the aromas of chicken paprika and spicy goulash swirled through my mind. My visits with Uncle Hans to his opera-loving friend Tony, who lived in "Little Italy," where I enjoyed the pasta dishes and the strong smells of garlic and cheese permeating that household, came to mind. I appreciated the freedom to be different, cherished the individuality the United States offered, and remembered it as being relatively free from government interference and regulation, except for the immigration officials who had made Papa return to Germany. I would describe in minute detail shopping with my mother on the broad thoroughfare of 86th street that ran from Central Park on the west, to Carl Schurz Park at the East River. The leaner our bodies became from the lack of food over the war years, the more Erika and my classmates and friends would urge me to recount tales of my island. I had walked it physically but relatively few times, mentally a thousand, ample for me to recall the magnificent architecture of the manmade stalagmites. Several of the maritime friends of my father and Uncle Hans, upon arriving in Hamburg during their travels before America had entered the war with Germany, had refreshed the ties to New York with gifts and momentoes. They always rekindled fond memories, so the images of my island were kept alive. I would tell of visiting the Aquarium, the Battery, Coney Island, racing on a mechanical horse through Steeplechase Park, or running into the waves at Brighton Beach. I had munched on hot dogs at Nathan's, admired the lions at the Central Park Zoo, made faces at the clowns in Ringling Brothers' circus at Madison Square Garden. I boasted of the rodeo, featuring cowboys and Indians, which was the most sought after topic, next to the interest in Hollywood.

The first opera I had ever attended in the old New York Metropolitan, had been "Hänsel and Gretel," by Engelbert Humperdinck. My music teacher in Hamburg, Hartwig Pahl, was also fascinated by my American stories, and called my lessons with him "destiny," because one of his own most influential teachers had been the composer of that beloved opera. Even my school teachers, and later, Hitler Youth leaders, were charmed by these accounts.

The Gypsy Fiddler.

During the time I had been in the children's home in Haffkrug, my parents had leased an acre of land, on which was situated a small vacation cottage, a hand-pumped well, and an outhouse. It was what Germans call a "Schrebergarten." Every inch of it was utilized to bring a maximum of produce. Mama had planted lettuce, tomatoes, cabbage, radishes, peas, carrots, beets, and beans. There were also four varieties of plum and cherry trees on the land. Dwarf apple and pear espalier fruit, and black and red current bushes lined the property on the east side, three different types of gooseberries on the west, and a hedge of raspberries to the north occupied most of the terrain. Lilac bushes on the south side constituted the only esthetic relief from this abundance of vegetation. I had missed the harvest of two long pyramid mounds that produced white asparagus, which were lovely to look at and to eat, if you cared for them. Germans love them as "Spargel und Schinken," a specialty item eaten with ham. I, however, was pleased to have been away at the time, and not having been urged to consume them. Up until the times food began to be scarce during the war, I still persisted in the finicky eating habits I had been permitted to indulge myself with during my younger years in the United States. My parents had never insisted in my eating any foods that I was not fond of, and I was still in the habit of rather going hungry than crossing my palate with anything that went against my grain. Sauerkraut, potato dumplings, carrots, and peppermint and chamomile teas were among those items I had not developed a liking for. Tante Auguste's enormous proportions came to mind, perhaps as a rationalization for my picky eating habits. I would compare hers arms with my thighs. Her stews and soups had really been very tasty, but she had the practice of always adding a large blob of schmalz or butter to her concoctions in the last minute. Although I have generally been blessed with a cast iron stomach, her cooking often caused me to up-chuck.

"The day will come when you will be happy to even have anything to eat," Papa had predicted. "Helen, your mother and I survived WW1 on a diet which consisted of almost 90% of Steckrüben (turnips). We don't want to live through another war on those rations. This piece of property is going to be a joint family effort at farming. After work and school, we will help Mama with the gardening."

These were the good intentions of my father. He put as much spare time as he could manage tending the garden, but compulsory overtime at the submarine base, together with his home workshop barter projects, soon diminished this to a trickle.

*　*　*

The first time I heard it , I believed it to be a phonograph record. No, such a sweet, clear sound could not come out of a scratchy machine, I said to myself. The sounds drifted across the fence from the adjoining yard, coming from the next door basement, which I thought to be vacant. As I craned my neck over the slotted back fence, I could see that the back door was open. I could make out the profile of a dark-haired man with finely chiseled features playing a violin. He was oblivious to all distractions around him, bowing his instrument with long, tender strokes, then sharp, repeated, short ones, the most beautiful gypsy melodies I had ever herd. Transfixed, I stood peering over the fence. When the music stopped, I applauded, then ducked so as not to be seen. The slender man stood in the doorway a moment longer, spoke quietly with someone I could not see through the fence slots, and disappeared.

That evening at the supper table, I told my parents of the beautiful music I had heard, and suggested that if they had been thinking of a Christmas present for me, a violin would be the ideal gift.

"If it is very expensive, I would gladly forego any other gifts for several years to come. I can chip in all my pocket money as well." I had been hoarding my allowance in a pair of socks, and had accumulated quite a small fortune, in my estimation.

Papa said, "We'll see what Santa Claus says."

That was mostly for Erika's benefit, I hoped. Santa Claus and the Easter Bunny were fun things to have believed in, but the disappointing realities had already made me depend on my parent's economic status for such acquisitions.

The imminence of the holiday reminded me once more how anxious I was to return to America. Our meager efforts had not resulted in any measure of success in achieving my objective, and I began to think of ways to improve our chances, perhaps with help from a higher power.

"Papa, the pastor at the Hauptkirche is giving instructions in the Lutheran faith to young people."

My father was astonished at my wanting to go for religious training without being urged to do so, for he had been forced to at an early age, and had resolved not to adapt the same policy with his own children.

"Your grandmother was always quoting the Bible. My brother, and sisters Betty and Else were herded to church several days during the week, as well as on Sundays."

"I would just like to ask some questions of the pastor. If he can't answer them, I'll have to make up my own mind about them," I replied.

"That's what each person has to decide for himself."

"The golden rule is what I try to live by," Mama added.

I thought of my father's favorite quote, "Where there's a will, there's a way," and how there still did not seem to be any obvious way to return home in spite of my fervent will.

I questioned my teacher on these slogans, including the "Gott mit uns" (god with us) inscription on the belt buckles of German soldiers.

"I don't think that God has anything to do with it, since it is man who is attacking man. It's therefor presumptuous to consider him to be with you for such undertakings."

I repeated these views to the pastor at the religious training sessions, but he was more reluctant to jeopardize his position with statements which the government would consider subversive. He tried to frame his responses in terms of abiding by the Ten Commandments in one's daily life, but I was having difficulties reconciling what I felt to be conflicting standards. I wanted to go back home, and temporal rules were imposing restrictions on me that were violating my rights of free choice. I decided that I would return to America if I would have to do it alone.

* * *

It had been just about the harvest time of our peaches when I had first heard the violin music. The following Sunday, we came home from our land in the country with a basket full of luscious fruit. Mama was canning much of it. I was eating some peaches in the backyard, when a voice came from across the fence saying, "Don't throw those pits away. I can use them for carving baskets and wooden shoes."

I was startled at first, but then realized it was the "Zigeuner Opa" (gypsy grandfather), our virtuoso neighbor. He later showed me some examples of his peach pit handiwork, adorable miniature baskets and wooden shoes. From then on, our family saved the peach pits for him, and also gave him some of our produce. The little boy living with him always acted like a shy fawn, looking at me with frightened brown eyes. He never spoke to me. I greeted them both whenever I saw them in the backyard or passed them on the street, but only the "Opa" acknowledged me. After he became aware of how much I enjoyed his music, he often played for me, repeating some of the "Zigeuner Weisen" I liked best. On my way to see my friend Irmgard, I would cross the Kibble Strasse, and pass him going to see some of his ethnic friends living there. Once in a while, a very Indian-looking woman clad in flowing fuchsia or kelly green saris visited our gypsy neighbors. Her dress was quite outstanding, but so also was a wart on her head the size of a large potato. The neighbors called her "Die Zigeunerin mit der Kartoffel auf dem Kopf" (the gypsy with the potato on her head). Sometimes she pushed an empty baby carriage, at other times she used it to transport goods. Once, I saw the shy boy sitting in it. I laughed when they passed by, and he jumped out and, running ahead of me, rang doorbells all along the Blücher Strasse. The irate occupants blamed me as I passed their doors, as the boy's Olympic sprinting had already taken him out of sight.

That Christmas I received a violin, and was enrolled with Hartwig Pahl, Music Pedagogue, whose home was on the Reeperbahn, on the corner of David Strasse. He accepted me as a student only after carefully looking me over, checking my fingers and my date of birth. As I fell in under the sign of Aquarius, and was only one day away from his own birthday, he permitted me to join his small group of students. I received one hour of instruction per week, but he demanded a minimum of two hours of practice daily, verified in writing by my parents each week during the initial six months. After this probationary period, I was on my own honor to put in the minimum practice time.

The musical tones of the violin are made by guiding the bow over the strings. The movement causes the strings to vibrate, giving off the most awful sounds until the student has managed the coordination of left hand finger placement, and long, smooth strokes. The memory of my first lesson is stamped on my mind like a cattle brand. Herr Pahl received me at the door, after which Frau Pahl ushered me into their spacious studio living room, which had a large green ceramic-tiled stove in one corner. In the winter, I could slowly warm up my instrument before the lesson began. A plush sofa stood against one wall, with a large oil painting of a wooded scene above it. There was a space for an electrified music stand next to a full-sized piano, with a death mask of Beethoven's grim features adorning the wall behind it. Two large windows overlooked the Reeperbahn, with a gigantic grandfather's clock separating them. On the wall opposite the sofa and piano stood an ornate glass-enclosed bookcase filled with leather-bound musical scores. Next to it, a huge carved oak desk, with a life-sized portrait of Hans von Bülow in formal evening wear over it.

"First, we will learn the notes on the line, 'es geht hurtig durch Fleiss,' " Herr Pahl said. "Then, in between the lines, 'frisch ans Clavier Emil.' " (The first letters of these German mnemonics indicate the notes in the music staff.) I was then given the third degree, "Quickly, Helen, what's the note on the fourth line?"

"D," I answered. He then proceeded to ask me questions in such quick succession that I became drenched in perspiration.

"Hold the violin like this- 'geh du alter Esel,' for the open strings."

I tucked the violin under my chin, and complained about the hardness against my shoulder. Tentatively, I stroked the open E string. Horrors- Beethoven's mask was crying! I could barely stand the screeching myself. My clammy fingers desperately tried to follow the instructions. Oh, gypsy, where did you ever get the skill to play so bewitchingly? I mentally vowed to practice only in the front living room at home, and never in my bedroom in the rear, so that the gypsy would not hear me until I mastered the instrument. The thought that perhaps I could some day play duets with my neighbor became my long- term goal.

Herr Pahl mentioned a black girl named Min, who was also taking violin lessons with him. She was the daughter of a hotel manager whom we occasionally saw on the trolley or city mass transportation. I often wondered what our teacher told her about me, for after a while, I had the feeling that he was spurring us on by arousing some competitive spirit between us.

"You two will be playing duets in no time. I just wonder who I will give the first violin part to." In the meanwhile, he also introduced me to another of his students, Elfriede, who already played the piano quite well. Chopin pieces were her specialty- the Beethoven mask looked down benevolently, perhaps even approvingly.

"Der Himmel voller Geigen" (The heavens full of Fiddles), was written down on a pad, like a doctor's prescription, by Herr Pahl. Dutifully, I walked to Benjamino's, a musty old music store with stacks of albums and sheet music taking up most of the rear part of the ancient establishment. The proprietor and his clerks were equally advanced in years. Solemnly, they took the piano and violin variety scores from behind dusty racks.

Every Saturday, Elfriede and I would practice duets together at her house. She, her parents and grandparents, lived in a large apartment on Valentine's Kamp, which was part of a huge pawn shop complex. These Saturday practice sessions became a delightful habit. We played the pieces Herr Pahl had helped us with, such as Träumerei, Largo by Händel, Minuet in G, and Hungarian dances. We made up our own programs for the holidays, when we had our parents listen to our progress. Elfriede's parents, as well as her grandfather, also played piano and violin. Sometimes they would join us in family musicales. Elfriede and I were steadfast in our practice sessions, stopping only after at least three hours to either play hide and seek in the warehouse section of that business, or to walk to the museums, botanical garden, or to go sleigh riding at the Stadtgraben (city moat) when it had snowed. She was an "A" student who never let you forget her accomplishments, bringing them up in subtle as well as obvious ways. She was a true over-achiever, I thought in the beginning, but realized that her domestic life with her grandparents brought on a precocious, star pet-of-the-roost attitude. She was a child intellectual. Her grandfather would discuss philosophy, poetry, and musical scores with her. When she recited Schiller poems to me, hesitating at certain lines, I would continue, and she would ask, "How did an American get to know that?" I would jokingly reply, "Haven't you heard of the New York school system? In Manhattan, German is only one small part of the culture."

I eventually made up my mind to have "Zigeuner Opa" listen to some of my practice pieces. The young boy had followed me to my teacher's studio several times, hiding in doorways on the way. When I became aware of him, he would dart ahead of me like a springbuck, zigzagging from one crevice to another. If I had failed to notice him, he would run by and tap me on the shoulder as he passed. I planned to ask Mama for some fruit from our garden to bring along for the gypsies, and then to mention my violin. Of course, the boy had already informed the "Opa" that I was taking violin lessons, having seen me leave to go to Elfriede's house with my black "machine gun case," as I called my violin case for the benefit of the neighborhood children. The ones that I did not care to associate with mockingly called me "Paganini."

My lesson was from five to six o'clock in the afternoon that Thursday. I walked home from the Reeperbahn, past some of the taverns, bars, and the all-ladies' band nightclub that were just starting business hours. It was always quite safe for women and children to stroll by that Broadway-type amusement center of Hamburg. Street crime was well controlled; muggers and child molesters were promptly hunted down with all the resources of the regime, which amounted to a very effective deterrent.

The women orchestra members of the club were just arriving.

"Keep on practicing, we can use you as soon as you want a job," the heavily made up leader had called to me as I walked by.

Mama had supper ready, awaiting only Papa's arrival from working overtime. At the table, I told them of my intention to visit the gypsies. They shared my opinion of the great musical skills of the "Opa," and agreed to let me drop by with some fruit for them the following day. After doing my homework and practicing, I went to bed, looking forward to demonstrating my progress to the Zigeuner.

The nights were now starting to be interrupted by the howling of air raid sirens announcing the approach of British bombers to the city limits. Occasional bombs had been dropped in our neighborhood. My family and our tenants would huddle together in our steel-post braced cellar hall until the all-clear sounded. That night, no bombers threatened, but I was awakened by the screams of the gypsy virtuoso and his grandson. Leaving the lights turned off, I pulled open the darkening shades and the window, and listened, the hair on my neck rising with fright.

"Los- raus, sofort mitkommen! Sie sind verhaftet!" (Go- get out, come along immediately! You are under arrest!) Staccato orders that I recognized again. No! Please don't let them be taken away! Why should they be taken to a labor camp, too? They surely have no skills that those S.S. men would need. They are hurting them! I can here it in the agonized shrieks! I closed the window, and buried my head under my pillow. I could not hear my parents in the next room. Erika did not wake up. The only sounds- my muffled sobs into the pillow, and the roar of a truck leaving. Then, silence. My only thought- Why?

Protesting "Heil Hitler."

The morning after the gypsies had been taken away, I said nothing about it to my parents. Mrs. Lubinski asked me in the hall if I had heard the commotion. Before going to school, I went by the gypsy's apartment. I really did not know what I hoped to find, but it was very important to me. Somehow, I hoped against hope that they would still be there. As I entered the dark hallway of the building, I heard sounds of sweeping. After knocking several times on the apartment door, a morose old woman asked gruffly what I wanted. I stammered, "I'm inquiring about the gypsy occupants."

"Good riddance! Look at the work left for me to clean up after them." Pausing, she leaned on the broom, looking me over. "What are they to you?"

"I live across the backyard from this house. I knew them from their music."

"Oh yes, your father is the American landlord," she muttered. "He has a workshop in his basement, and is always blowing fuses! What's he making in there?"

"I don't know," was my reply, for her tone was quite hostile.

She gestured wildly with the broom, "Those darn gypsies! What terrible tenants they were, not like the nice, neat people your father has."

She rambled on about the virtues of good housekeeping and cleanliness, pointing at the untidiness of the room with her broom. "Hitler is doing the right thing! Put people like that to work! How can we have an orderly society without pulling together, eh?" She came right up to me, pinning me to the wall with her eyes.

"Did you ever hear the gypsy's violin playing?" I asked timidly.

"Your clothes, are they from America?" she asked in return.

I looked at myself to check on what I was wearing. I was still numb from the experience of the night raid. With tears streaming down my face, I turned away from her, and walked to school on a different street so as to avoid contact with any of my classmates.

For two days afterwards, I could not pick up my violin without bursting into tears. I did not go to meet Elfriede that Saturday for our usual practice session, and the following day I became ill with a severe ear infection. Elfriede came for a visit while I was recuperating, as did Irmgard. I did not tell them about the disappearance of the gypsies, because I could not be certain of their attitudes, since their fathers were members of the N.S.D.A.P. I was becoming more and more leery of the ubiquitous uniformed men; the plaques in stores insisting on the Nazi greeting "Heil Hitler" were quite offensive to me. I protested obliquely by calling "Good Day" upon entering shops or other business establishments.

Eventually, I told Herr Pahl about the abduction of the gypsies. He opened the window nearest the piano, sat down and played "The Moldau" by Smetternach, a melody prohibited by the regime. When he finished, he closed the casement loudly, exclaiming, "How stupid they are, not even recognizing a forbidden composition! In your "Heaven Full of Violins" music book, the piece "Colnidre" is also on the banned list. I will play that for you, too, but to be safe, only by myself. He played it, and then went to his desk to pull out a document from the Reichsmusik Kammer (National Music Board). He wrote my name on the formidable paper and handed it to me. "Here is your release from Hitler Youth duty. You have to devote all your spare time to the study of music, and are now officially exempt from having to attend any of their meetings."

How fortunate I was to have that document in my possession, for the following week, the crosseyed Gruppen Führerin again appeared on our doorstep. Triumphantly, Mama handed her the document, which she snatched, read, and slammed the outside door shut as she left in a fury. I was fortunate enough never to be urged to participate in any Hamburg Hitler Youth activities thereafter.

* * *

Papa had arranged for me to be sent to the Lüneburger Heide, the tranquil heather country, to another children's resort home open to Howaldt Werft employees, this time in Weihe. With a pink travel ticket around my neck, violin case in one hand, small suitcase in the other, and dressed in red, white, and blue, I was ready to take the train from Altona. We met most of my fellow camp mates at the Hauptbahnhof Hamburg, and then continued on to either Jesteburg or Bucholz, depending on the connecting train. Upon arrival, a long but beautiful walk through pine forests and heather fields dotted with cedar and slender birch trees was most enchanting. Bedecked with a Loden coat, shepherd's hat and cane, Herr Rothman guided us to a tile-roofed mansion nestled in a flower garden. A wheat field was situated across from the house, and pine trees obscured the nearest neighbors, who were apparent only upon close inspection. These two residences were almost always vacant, we later determined. As we turned into the property, we were overwhelmed by a most unusual sound.

I there was confronted with my first close-up encounter with a peacock, posed like the top model in a fashion show. His crested head jerked from side to side, his electric blue neck rolled in uniform rhythm, and his magnificent tail fanned out in full splendor. Each time the peacock unfurled his colorful pride, pivoting as if for applause, it sounded like the crackling of the shifting of an old auto clutch. His strut was not hurried, but artfully synchronized; since he is virtually inedible, I imagine he felt quite secure, and born to be heard as well as seen. The hens were less gaudy, also crested like the cocks, but in more subdued earth colors. They seemed to be immune to the show-off's prancing, but I was utterly fascinated.

Schwester Lina touched my shoulder, then took the violin case from my hand. Herr Rothman directed the boys into forming a line, ready to enter their rooms in the home. Our suitcases arrived in a horse-drawn wagon, which had gone on ahead of us. The help carried them into the building. A large glass-enclosed veranda was situated on one side of the structure; at the rear was an outside staircase leading to the girl's dormitory. This place was to become my peaceful retreat. We swam in the swift current of the river Seeve, which was lined by peat moss bogs, made long marches through forest and heather country, yet hardly ever encountering another soul that was not connected with the home. We did visit the most impressive, courtly mansion of an artist couple, a sculptor and artist who had created their own private museum in this wilderness.

I had promised Herr Pahl that I would conscientiously practice my violin daily, however, I was the only one who had brought an instrument along. Every afternoon, we had to have a two hour rest period. I managed to persuade Schwester Lina to permit me to practice in the forest during this time slot. I used to set up my music stand firmly on the pine needle ground, and practice my Wohlfahrt Etudes (Welfare exercises). I had teased my mother about this title, saying, what a shame it was that I was on welfare at my age. I fiddled every day while the rest of the children, as well as the help had their naps. Only once that I knew of, was I ever overheard. A shepherd looking for a stray happened to come upon me. I don't know how long he had been listening before he called attention to himself by clearing his throat. My bow screeched to a halt; he tipped his hat and disappeared through the trees.

My first stay in Weihe was for a period of four weeks during school vacation. Our daily routine was pretty much the same as in Haffkrug, except that the sounds and briny scent of the sea were replaced by the hush and fragrance of the heather. After our bed-making and rigorous morning exercises, we had our breakfasts. I became friends with the head nurses Schwester Lina and Schwester Margot, who were in charge of the home at different times. Herr Rothman was either the owner or manager of the establishment, and his wife ran the kitchen with an iron hand.

The stillness of the environment was broken only by either the cries of the watchful peacock, or the effervescent clamor we were prone to. Long hikes into the interior of the pine-scented forests and rolling sandy paths with acres of purple heather touching the horizon filled our afternoons. On rainy days, we sat around the long dining room tables, or clustered together in the glass-enclosed veranda, singing of the countryside that we had explored just before being driven to shelter by the elements. We learned the text of "Im Wald und auf der Heide," "Wenn alle Brünnlein fliessen," "Wem Gott will rechte Gunst erweisen," "Auf der Lüneburger Heide," and many more. Before meals, we said grace to thank God for our food.

Hitler Attends the "Bismarck" Commissioning.

My father had to work longer and longer overtime hours on the submarines. The short times that he was able to be at home he spent in his shop making the wooden bowls and cart wheel spokes he felt would be good barter products. He was convinced that, in the event that the war would become protracted, money would no longer be the most useful trading medium. The air raids were becoming more frequent, and bunkers were being built, but were not yet ready to receive the neighborhood populations. Papa installed additional adjustable pipe supports in the basement hall, broke a hole through the wall connecting us to our neighbor's cellar, and bricked it over with a thin veneer which could easily be pushed over in an emergency. The howling of air raid sirens was no longer an occasional happening.

In the beginning, it was a very exciting event; the tracer rounds of the Flak looked like beautiful fireworks. Spellbound, we stood in the dark room, looking out the back window to watch the green and red luminescent beads find their targets centered in the beams of search lights honing in for the kill. Crews could be seen parachuting from the hapless aircraft disabled by the intense cross firing. Only then did I begin to realize the seriousness of the scenes. We tore ourselves away from those deadly spectacles, and dashed down stairs to join our tenants in the basement, hoping to escape injury or death from bombs or shrapnel. Mrs. Lubinski,

Mrs. Kröger, and Peter always joined us in our private bunker. Mr. Lubinski was away at sea. Herr and Frau Becher occasionally came to cower with us; like ostriches, we buried our heads under blankets whenever an explosion was heard.

In the early part of the war, the bombs were still relatively small. A direct hit to a house could still leave a well-braced basement intact, with rescue from the outside a possibility, I was assured. Seeing the destruction already wrought by those "small" bombs left me totally unconvinced. The first bomb to strike our neighborhood was a direct hit on the pub my father usually sent me to for his occasional ½ liter of Alster Wasser, a local concoction of lemon soda and beer, which was his favorite summer refreshment. The sight of the totally demolished Gastwirtschaft became a local curiosity, at least until the Angriffe (attacks) became more intensive.

Scores of prisoners of war, as well as other imported labor, worked on the building sites of the neighborhood bunkers. The one we were to be assigned to was located at the intersection of Schaumburg Strasse and Johannes Strasse. It was about four stories high, with portholes for ventilation, and of heavy steel reinforced concrete construction. Three inch steel doors were yet to be installed. Nighttime raids were becoming supplemented by daylight attacks. One time, on my way home from school, I did not make it home in time to reach our own shelter. I tried to take cover in a circular, turret-type bomb shelter. The doors were not wide enough to accommodate the mad rush of people trying to get inside. A British plane swooped down to strafe the throng still outside, which consisted largely of women and children. I had sought shelter crouching in an entryway across the street, and observed the melee during the firing. Two men ran over fallen bodies to dive headlong into the bunker entrance. I remained in the entryway to avoid the panic of the crowd. My school briefcase stood next to me, containing my books and the bomb and Flak shrapnel I had been collecting and trading. This had become a hobby with most of the children, with bomb fragments being the more highly prized. After this raid, I gave my collection away to Karl-Heinz, a neighborhood boy, and never sought any reminders of the war again. We were urged by radio, newspaper, and teachers, never to pick up any colorful toys or celluloid pen and pencil sets lying in the streets, for the enemy was dropping booby traps loaded with explosives.

* * *

Inasmuch as Hamburg was a Hanseatic League city, many of its ancient laws were still observed. The Nazi system could, or perhaps did not, quite penetrate the setup of the educational structure of the Oberbau, which conducted a one week long testing procedure for student aspirants from all over the city. Of the 42 students in my class, five had been groomed by Fräulein Plaas to be part of the chosen few to be considered for admission to the highly rated free facility. I was one of the lucky three that passed the exams from our school. Elfriede had also entered the competition, fretting quite unnecessarily, for she was required only to take the three day written test, which she easily passed. Due to certain academic weaknesses of mine, particularly in math, I was required to make up these deficiencies by scoring high on oral and physical tests. My teacher later informed me, since she was on the testing council, that my recital of the poem of my choice had been the deciding factor in my case. "Nis Randers" by Otto Ernst, to this day, is one of my favorite and, I feel, most touching epics of the sea.

* * *

"Well, America, you are invited!" Irmgard's father said to me one day. "You are coming with Irmgard and me to the commissioning of the "Bismarck," the most powerful battleship afloat."

I was not particularly enthusiastic, which he noticed.

"What happened to your interest in inspecting ships?" he asked.

"I would much prefer to look over the sail training ship "Gorch Fock."

He laughed, "We lost a sailor in you, too bad you're not a boy."

"Not just a sailor,' I countered, a captain or an admiral would be better."

"Well," he said, "the reason I'm inviting you is that the Führer will be coming. This will probably be one of the most historical events you will ever be privileged to witness!"

I had suspected as much, but my dread of the expected crowds made me shudder in anticipation. I tried to beg off politely, using the excuse of not being comfortable in standing in one spot for hours as an acceptable reason. I can still recall the surprised expression on his face.

Several days before the commissioning on August 24th, 1940, my teacher, Frl. Plaas made the announcement in class, "Girls, you will have the day off to attend this event. The Führer will be there to officiate. This new 45,000 ton battleship has eight 15-inch guns, and will be used to raid the Atlantic shipping lanes."

Irmgard and I met at the movies the Sunday before. "I will be coming along after all, please tell your father."

We left Irmgard's house on the morning of the big event. Her father wore his brown uniform with the swastica armband. He walked in front of us, his shiny black boots clicking in staccato rhythm. His large frame loomed before us with an air of self-importance. The closer we got to the waterfront, the more people joined us. Every available male Party member in the entire city was streaming towards, not only the Landungsbrücken, but also the entire park area near the Bismarck statue. Rimmed in brown, hands clasped across their chests, linked to the next man with a leather belt, the Party members formed a human chain. Forming additional rows behind them stood first the Hitler Youth boys, and then the girls (B.D.M.).

Irmgard and I were clad in summer dresses. My father could not attend because he could not be released from his work, which was essential to the war effort. Mama and Erika remained at home.

I spotted Herr Becher, strutting like the peacock in Weihe, trying to get the attention of anybody.

He noticed me, too. "So, my landlord's daughter, das Gnädige Fräulein (gracious young lady) is coming to see the Führer," he jested loudly.

Oh, how I disliked that man! I tried not to show it, and just nodded curtly to him. The motorcade of the Führer and his entourage was due around 11:00am. Irmgard and I were permitted to stand behind the first line of men; the boys were in back of us. There was much kidding going on. Irmgard's father had mentioned that I was an American. He hoped that I could be trusted not to attempt to assassinate the beloved Führer. The men and boys around me laughed and said that they would keep a careful eye on me. As the United States was not yet involved in the European conflict, most people were cordial to me. My tall, Aryan appearance helped.

The three human chains holding the crowds back reached from the harbor to well past the wide chaussee of the Bismarck statue. I was an incredible sight. Like the beads of a brown necklace, the S.A. stood on both sides of the street, the boys with their brown shirts and black shorts dutifully vigilant behind them. The girls, the Bund Deutscher Mädel, dressed in white starched blouses with the same neck scarves as the fellows, but wearing black skirts, brought up the rear guard.

I stared in amazement; people were standing, sitting, crouching and otherwise hovering around the pedestal of the mighty stone Bismarck, as well as in trees, park bridge overhangs, balconies, rooftops, windows, and doorways. The sloping lawns, paths, and benches were covered with what appeared to be the majority of the population of Hamburg. The vessel itself could not be seen from our vantage point. Red Cross stations were set up between the harbor and the sculpted Iron Chancellor. Irmgard and I first stood, then leaned, and finally squatted against the legs of the Hitler Youth boys. It was now almost 1:00pm. The motorcade was to stop near us, with Hitler stationed just a few feet away.

"I have to go to the bathroom, Irmgard," I announced.

She explained to her father that we would head for the nearest comfort station. We squeezed past the human bands with great difficulty, and rushed to the toilets, only to encounter long lines. As I stood at the edge of the park area, the memory of gatherings at Madison Square Garden events seemed like a minute group of people, in comparison to the ubiquitous human carpet spread out before me. I was completely overwhelmed to find such crowds about me. After leaving the ladies' room, I dallied, not really anxious to return to my allotted spot in the midst of the human chains.

"Let's walk up a little further, and skirt the road the car of the Führer will take," I said, but Irmgard insisted that we go back. Just then, a motorcycle holding a sign anticipating the restlessness I felt roared by. "Er kommt," (he's coming) it read.

We elbowed our way through the crowds, squeezing past the now somewhat tiring lines, who were miraculously reviving at the news of Hitler's imminent arrival. After what still seemed like hours, a tremendous roar of human voices began to engulf us like a tidal wave. It started from the high inland slope, and gained momentum until it reached a deafening crescendo all about us: Heil!, Heil!, Heil! The modern Caesar in his limousine chariot drove slowly past the chanting, enthralled masses of admirers. The world before me had turned into a Hollywood extravaganza. I could not believe I was facing reality.

He was hailed as a God. No man should receive such adulation, I thought. It was a warm day, women had been fainting, and the Red Cross had been busy reviving or tending the heat or emotion stricken victims. Irmgard and her father were obviously completely awe struck. The motorcade stopped near us, then continued a little further. Hitler was standing in the limousine, just close enough for me to see his eyes. I shuddered at his glance, feeling a chill running down my spine. He stepped out of the vehicle, and walked towards the piers; we could no longer see him or see the vessel when he made his presentation. Loudspeakers had been set up at various locations to carry his speech to the entire assemblage, but I must confess that I do not remember much of the contents of his message. That evening, it was re-broadcast over the radio for all the nation to hear. His battle cry is well documented.

Once in action, the "Bismarck" sank the British battle cruiser "Hood", and severely damaged a new battleship off the coast of Greenland. The great "sink the Bismarck" hunt was on with every available British warship joined in a 1,750 mile chase; aircraft attacks, five destroyers firing at it all night, and the combined forces of two battleships and a cruiser finally sent her to the bottom on May 27th, 1941, 400 miles off the coast of France.

Gestapo Close Call.

My mother's ties to Pinneberg were quite strong, and we would often visit Erna, who was not only a super housewife and gardener, but a furrier with creative design talent. Her husband Henry raised rabbits as a hobby; he had gone to school with Mama. Erna's mother, Tante Paula to me, was somehow related to my great-grandmother, who had been born in Prussia. She told stories of Russian atrocities similar to the ones related by Oma, my father's mother. In trying to visualize the long train of ancestors, the baggage car goes back to the East on both sides of my parent's families.

I was hoping to get to Königsberg for a visit to Tante Hildegard, my Jewish godmother, the wife of the friend of my father who had left the United States during the depression because of lack of work. However, she was only able to send me one last postcard before being sent to a concentration camp. Uncle Richard's letter to us from the Russian front spoke of his fears that his wife had been killed, while he had been conscripted to defend the system responsible for his wife's death.

"It would be so easy to just step in the way of a Russian bullet," was the last sentence of that letter.

I was invited to come to Kiel. Mama brought me to the Altonaer Hauptbahnhof, and I was deposited into the Schnellzug (rapid train). On the trip, I became enraptured with a Feldwebel (Sergeant) and a university professor who shared the compartment, and my snacks, with me, while I spread the gospel of utopian America.

"Once my country enters the war, Germany might as well give up!" I told the handsome soldier. The professor laughed at my childish remark, and I countered with, "Since you are at the pinnacle of education, why is there war at all?"

The two men argued and discussed this point from the military and idealistic standpoints of their respective professions, while I listened intently. Their presentations were eloquent, but the cliches were the same as I had heard on both shores in family kitchens and living rooms.

My father's sister Tante Betty and her husband Herbert were waiting for me at the Kieler Bahnhof. They were much amused seeing me escorted off the train on the arm of the professor, with a Feldwebel as a porter for my luggage. "Not yet a teenager," Uncle Herbert grinned, "and already an entourage!"

Tante Else, my father's youngest sister, was also one of the Kielers. She was married to Uncle Albert, one of the drollest, most gemütlich of men I have ever met. He was a lifelong employee of the Kieler Utility Company. All four of these relatives shared a mutual interest in sports. They belonged to the Kieler Turnverein, participated in gymnastics, jogging, swimming, long and short distance bicycling, kayak racing, and camping. The two men had built their own paddle boats, and were also members of the local kayak club. I was taught how to ride a bicycle, and learned how to paddle, a skill I once used to brazenly challenge the right of way of a steamship in the Kieler Harbor, which is on the Baltic Sea. We camped on a remote island in the Plöner See, negotiating some quite choppy eddies on the way. I insisted on having an open umbrella over me to prevent spiders from dropping on me from the crevices in the tent. We took bike trips through Schleswig Holstein, and visited Friedrichsruh, Bismarck's former estate.

Spazieren and Wandern, terms which have become familiar in English speaking countries, were my favorite means of getting from one place to another, and have become lifelong disciplines. As most other means of public transportation were frequently not available due to disruptive bombings, my legs were kept in good condition out of necessity. I was happy with the fanaticism for sports in the two households, hoping that I would learn to be a better participant in the annual Sports festivals held in Hamburg.

Water sports were continued on weekends, with excursions to the Kieler Harbor. Uncle Herbert was a marine engineer, and had trained as a cadet on board the "Gorch Fock," one of the sail training ships of the German navy. We were invited for afternoon coffee and a tour of the ship. I scrambled up a few rungs of the rigging, and tried out a hammock, wondering if I could get used to sleeping in one. The sister ship to the "Gorch Fock," the "Horst Wessel," which was usually stationed in Stetin, also lay in the harbor. She is now our American "Eagle," the war prize used by the U.S. Coast Guard for sail training cadets, and is stationed in New London, Connecticut.

My other grandmother, the original Memel or Klaipeda native, had also invited me to stay with her while I was in Kiel. My uncles thought her to be most eccentric, and my aunts actually feared her. Papa and Uncle Hans had supported Oma, giving her financial assistance up until she died, the year after I stayed with her on my vacation. She had come for a visit to Hamburg soon after we had settled in the apartment house. Her stay had been brief, and therefor her habits and lifestyle were not familiar to me. She was a lean, straight dark-haired woman who wore old-fashioned feathered hats with high crowns, dark dresses, and used a cane to walk with. When we first met, she had shaken hands with me and commented about the family resemblance to my grandfather. We were yet to become really acquainted.

Tante Betty and I carried my luggage from the Ring Strasse where she lived to the old part of Kiel where my grandmother lived. After a twenty minute walk, we entered a wide Torweg which opened to a large cultivated garden, and walked along the path on the edge of it to a small building attached to an apartment house. I remember thinking that it had perhaps been built during George Washington's time. The ancient door was opened after my aunt called "Mutter" several times. We were ushered into a kitchen that looked like the staging in the opera "Hänsel and Gretel." She had come to the door assisted by her cane; a table had been set for three, and after greeting me with a handshake and a kiss on the forehead, she urged us to sit down. The decorative, rose adorned porcelain coffee pot came out only to fill the china cups, disappearing under a blue satin lace trimmed cosy, which kept the pot warm between refills. Elaborate petits-fours and fruit tarts were on display platters, and open-faced, dainty sandwiches with fish, eggs, cucumbers, and tomatoes sprinkled with chive and parsley were appetizingly displayed.

I sat down eagerly, and thoroughly enjoyed the marinated herring and tiny shrimp sandwiches, while Tante Betty and Oma talked about the war.

"How are you able to get to a shelter before the bombs begin to fall?" Tante Betty asked.

"I have this carriage," Oma replied, pointing to an old-fashioned perambulator standing in the corner next to the door. "I can lean on it as I walk. It's filled with clothes and my important documents."

We all ate some of the delicious cakes, and then Tante Betty excused herself to Oma, gave me a hug, and called out, "Auf Wiedersehn! See you both Friday," as she disappeared through the well worn door.

My arms wilted in my lap; the moments passed as I fidgeted nervously in my seat. I looked up into her tired, unfamiliar face, at the fine lines etched around her animated eyes. Oma was studying me just as carefully, her gaze inched across my form like a probing machine. Her unsmiling features could not reveal to me what emotions were stirring in her. After my initial interest, my eyes began to wander, to investigate the furniture, cupboards, hearth, and broom standing in a corner, when a black cat jumped up to the open window from the garden. I was convinced that my Oma was a witch.

"We will go to church tonight," were the first words to break the silence. She started collecting the rest of the dishes which had been left on the table; most of them had been gathered by Tante Betty automatically, and previously deposited near the large old sink. I jumped up and asked if she wanted me to wash or dry them.

Her answer, "Abtrocknen (dry)!" came after handing me a long linen dish towel with the initials M.A. embroidered on it.

After we finished with the dishes, she handed me a well worn Bible, motioned to the chair I had been sitting in, and commanded, "Hinstzen und lesen (sit and read)!" Dutifully, I sat down and opened the book.

"Der Herr ist Treu, der wird euch stärken und bewahren vor dem Argen," I read aloud.

Oma came hobbling over to my chair, patted me on the shoulder, saying, "He will, He will. I know it!"

Slowly, I closed the Bible, and wondered at the random opening.

We went to church that night, where just a few old women and one child in the congregation sat listening to a brief prayer. There was no music or pageantry, just a united appeal led by the pastor. Slowly, we filed out of the house of worship. I tried to support Oma's free arm and help her down the stairs, but she would have none of it.

"I'll manage by myself, thank you," she said fiercely. "I've done so all my life."

Several of the women had gathered, and were waiting for her to descend the steps. I was proudly introduced, and shook hands with all. They in turn patted and stroked me on the head.

The following morning, I was allowed to go into the garden, which was a collective effort of several of the tenants in the main building. Oma' house was just a small "Anbau" (appurtenance); like she, a self contained unit. She had planted some herbs, a few tomato plants, lettuce, beans, and carrots.

"We will go to the market after breakfast," she announced.

Her baby carriage was emptied of clothes and documents, which were temporarily stored on her bed. She pushed the vehicle out to the Torweg, and I trudged along as slowly as possible.

At the market, many of the women I had met at the church the night before had their own stands set up, and were busy exchanging their wares for currency and rationing cards. One of them gave Oma extra berries and some Fall Obst (windfall fruit), which she made into jam or dried after we had returned to her house. I had brought books and a ball along from home. I read and played some of the games I had learned in Hamburg. These were apparently different in Kiel, as I found when some giggling neighborhood girls drew my attention to them. Joining in with them, I had a fun, albeit raucous afternoon, until a group of rowdy boys interrupted our play. They ran off with Oma's carriage, which she had left standing outside the kitchen door. To my surprise, Oma made a lively sprint out through the Torweg, her cane in one hand, and the corn broom in the other, but she was no match for the boys. I grabbed the broom from her, and dashed after the bullies, thrashing wildly at the one that was pushing her pram. The others did not interfere, and the vehicle was safely returned to Oma' kitchen corner.

After dinner, all the dishes were washed, dried, and neatly stacked in the cupboard. We swept and mopped the kitchen. She smoothed her straight, black hair, which had just the slightest touch of grey, put on a freshly starched white apron over her dark blue dress, and sat by a lamp reading aloud from her Bible. Unless we went to services at the church, this ritual was observed for ten or fifteen minutes every evening. When the Bible was closed, she would bring out the family album with pictures of my uncle and father in sailor suits, of my father in a cowboy outfit, and Tante Betty and Tante Else in gym clothes hanging from parallel bars or rings, or riding bicycles. The cat would lie on my lap with eyes closed, purring softly, momentarily blinking when I reached to turn a page. Two questions were foremost on my mind, but it took me several days to get up enough courage to ask them.

After breakfast, Oma announced that she had a special treat for me. She went to the pantry, and came back with a large bowl full of dried pieces of bread crusts, some of which looked months old, and moldy.

I looked at her questioningly, but she just said, "Put on your sweater and cap. We are going to the Stadtgraben." She placed her handbag and the bowl of bread into the carriage, and we trekked out to the moat of the city park to the beat of her own cadence.

"I go to feed them several times a year," she explained, "but the streets have less and less refuse these days. Soon there will be none, if the war continues much longer."

It was a beautiful, bright and clear day, and I really did not need any head covering, but she had seen the scar from my mastoid operation, and insisted that I wear my hat. She wore a black straw hat trimmed with a single white flower. I am certain that they recognized her, for no sooner had I seen them, when they stopped their preening and stretching, and flocked around her.

Swans, those stately water birds, with their long graceful necks, greeted an old friend. I was overwhelmed by the trust and interest the pen displayed, showing off its cygnets, and the cob respectfully watching, while Oma fed the mother by hand.

She spoke to them softly, "Kommt nur, ihr Schönen."

I felt like an intruder, and slowly moved to the park bench, so as not to interrupt this idyllic scene. Oma called to me, and soon I was also feeding the bolder ones. The cygnets were kept at a proper distance from me by the father of the brood. When the bowl was empty, we sat down on the park bench, the birds retreated to the water, and after a while, I got up the courage to ask one of the questions that had been on my mind for a very long time.

"How did Papa lose his eye?" I inquired.

She looked at me for what seemed like an eternity. I saw tears form in her eyes, and I was sorry to have brought up the subject. She wiped her eyes with the snow white handkerchief she had retrieved from her bag, swallowed, adjusted her hat, gazed at the water fowl, and began her explanation. "Erich always took the same route to school, but on his way home, he would explore another neighborhood, mostly in the vicinity of the harbor. He loved the ships and the water. One of the beautiful homes near the Admiralty had a large nut tree in the yard. Your father remembered this tree, and decided to gather some of the nuts, as the owner of the house never picked any of them. A fence surrounded the grounds, and although he could easily have climbed over it, he did not. Several nuts had fallen to the ground, and were within reach of the fence. He took a twig, lay down on the ground, and attempted to snare some from under the fence. One large walnut looked particularly inviting, and as he pulled it closer to his face to gather it, it exploded. That explosion caused the loss of his eye."

I was stunned at her words, and asked how it could be legal for someone to plant explosives in a yard. "What kind of horrible person would find it necessary to protect a few nuts in such a fashion?" I thought of the flowers I had picked so often from some neighbor's yard on my way home from school in Bethpage.

My mother had referred to me as the notorious flower snatcher, when I presented her with a bouquet.

"Don't go into someone else's property," she had admonished me, and I thereafter looked for wild blossoms of clover, violet, and forget-me-nots along the sides of the roads instead.

We started our journey back to Oma's house, and a few blocks from the Torweg, the same rowdy boys ran past us, taunting Oma about her hobble and the carriage.

"Hexe (witch)!" they called.

At first, she said nothing, and when I became angry at their behavior, she shouted at them, "One more step towards us, and you will get it with this!" She brandished her cane threateningly towards the boys, and they disbursed.

We reached home just as the air raid alarm sounded. Oma quickly transferred her clothes and documents from the bed to her carriage, and we hurried off to the Luftschutzkeller (air raid shelter).

* * *

My parents had been extremely productive while I was gone. Proudly, Mama showed me the neatly lined shelves of vegetables, preserved fruits, jams, and her latest crop of black currants stored in juice form. Papa had purchased a hog with two of his co-workers from Howaldt shipyard, and they had butchered it in secrecy out in the country. I was not told about this until years later, as the death penalty was imposed for such unauthorized deeds. I was delighted at the amount of additional meat we suddenly had available to us. Although I suspected that it was pork, my mother explained that it was horsemeat she had obtained "Vierfach auf Marken", which meant that one could obtain four times the usual quota if one took advantage of the substitution.

My father's workshop was set up like a miniature production line, and between his commuting by ferry to Neuhof, where he put in 12 to 14 hours a day working on the base, we only got to have conversations at mealtimes. He had to neglect his hobbies of chess and swimming, and once again became a workaholic. He was lamenting about the lack of a certain machine that would be useful for one phase of his production setup, but he had already bartered his diamond ring and gold watch for other pieces of equipment.

"Our country property," he proposed, "combined with the cash I'm earning with my overtime, would pay for the saw I need."

Mama was adamant about the value of this productive piece of land. "Besides all the food we have been harvesting, the cottage would be ideal as emergency housing!"

Papa's argument was that they had already made up ample provisions for our survival, and the possibility that our house, which was in the middle of a working class neighborhood, would be bombed, was in the low percentage range.

"They are after the industrial areas, the shipyards, factories, and submarine pens. Those are the targets they will concentrate on!"

We always discussed the possibilities of all the other countries which would attack Germany, and of course we estimated that if the U.S. entered the conflict, the war would be quickly brought to a finish. I was learning European history in school, and spoke with horror about the Thirty Years' War. A friend of mine, a girl of Norwegian descent, and I also debated the length of the war on the way to and from the orthopedic exercise class we were required to attend. Our class always stimulated our appetites, but without ration cards, we were limited to only three items we could afford with our limited allowances. We gorged ourselves on dill pickles, sauerkraut, or synthetic sodas we drank in the warm weather, or the artificial "Glühwein" (mulled wine) to warm us in the winter months.

Papa's persistence eventually won out. The Schrebergarten Pachtland was sold, and a brand new circular saw with various interchangeable blades was now standing in one corner of the shop. He had stopped chain smoking a long time ago, and used his and Mama's cigarette rations to invest in lumber. He was looking forward to Sunday in great anticipation as the day to try out his new gadget. Mama, Erika, and I were in the kitchen busy preparing the Sunday noon dinner, which was now our only complete family gathering mealtime. The table was set, and Mama was putting the last seasoning into the gravy, when she asked me to summon my father. I was about to open the shop door, when I heard an odd whirr, followed by a loud thump and a cry of pain from Papa above the sound of the motors. Mama had heard it as well, and was already behind me as I opened the door. She ran ahead of me, pulled the plug of the saw, and instantly wrapped the dish towel she had in her hand around Papa's jaw. The towel was immediately soaked in blood. We eased Papa to the floor, where he passed out. I fetched some more towels, and gasped as Mama lifted her dishcloth to put fresh linens onto the wound. She tried to replace the flesh around the jaw where the shattered circular saw blade had penetrated, push his jaw back into place, and keep firm pressure on the wound to stem the flow of blood.

I rushed to our tenant Frau Lubinski, who summoned the police to drive my parents to the Kiefer Klinik in Hamburg. Blood was all over the shop floor, saw, and walls. At least twenty of my father's teeth lay between wood chips, or hung exposed out of his mouth. The amount of blood loss made me fearful for my father's very life. Erika and I huddled on the sofa waiting for my mother to return from the clinic.

She came back late that evening. Papa will be fine, as good as new in no time, we were told. He had to remain in the hospital for several weeks, and upon his return, only a relatively thin scar remained of the terrible gaping wound I had seen earlier. Several doctors had worked on him for hours, and skillfully restored his good looks.

* * *

Every spring, district schools held sports competitions. My grade in the Schomburg School in Altona met in a large field in the "Allee." It was, in effect, a miniature olympic event. Irmgard, and later Efriede, put themselves in a frenzy of preparation to achieve the various goals and plateaus. The repetition of calisthenics and dance to music were the only forms of exercise I really enjoyed. Dance at that time not being encouraged, I practiced in secret. I attended these hot, raucus, and crowded school events with little enthusiasm. My teacher, Frl. Plaas, noticed my lack of participation. My parents received a letter concerning this matter from the school council, recommending that I attend weekly lessons in orthopedic exercises in a beautifully equipped gym in the Museum Strasse, to work out three times weekly with mostly tall boys and girls who had developed some form of backaches.

My new friend Mariane and I were again doing our orthopedic exercises, swinging our custom length broomsticks.

"Like every good witch apprentice has to!" I would joke, and then lament, "Verdammt noch mal, this better be really beneficial to us!" We commiserated about our height together, calling each other, "Storch im Salat (stork in salad)!"

My arms and legs were automatically programming themselves to the rhythm of the "eins, zwei, drei" chant of our teacher. My mind wandered from the Museum Strasse gym out to either a sunny ocean scene, or to my Manhattan Island, and clicked back to my immediate surroundings after each set of movements. We bombarded our instructor with questions doubting the value of what to us was merely torture. She assured us that the exercises would prove beneficial. The only immediate results we could measure was the increase in our appetites, and the dubious value of our pickle and sauerkraut diet.

The next Sportfest was to be held in one month, and we anticipated that we would have to make a good showing. My athletic activities had to be in competition with my music, though, so together with my Saturday practice sessions with Elfriede, my time was carefully rationed.

A pretty, redhaired girl name Hannelore (which was a very popular name at that time) was to take part in the running and "Geländespiele" (country games) of the Hitler Youth Sportfest. She invited me to come along on the overnight camp-out in tents. I was delighted with this prospective adventure, but my mother saw political overtones involved, and refused to let me go. My ranting was quite loud, and as I slammed the front door to walk off my anger, I ran into Herr Becher lurking in the hallway. We took pains to avoid him whenever possible, but several times Papa had noticed him surreptitiously spying on us. It would not be long before we would know the reason for his behavior.

I hurried over to Hannelore's apartment one block away.

"My mother doesn't want me to go to the meet," I blurted out to her father, who was also a musician. I had gotten to know the family quite well, and felt that I could unburden myself and gain their sympathy and support. He and his wife never refused their daughter anything, I thought. "Well, Mama is afraid that my earache will return if I should get chilled, and the weather has been quite damp and nasty lately."

To my dismay, Hannelore's mother agreed. "Perhaps Hannelore would also be better off to stay at home, especially since she has been having the sniffles lately."

Hannelore let out a loud wail, and I decided to leave expeditiously. By the time I reached our house, my anger had subsided.

My mother remarked again, "I just don't trust those Hitler Youth leaders, with their sadistic notions of Abhärten. They may have you playing outside in the rain, or even have forced marches to toughen you, as they say."

The following Monday, Hannelore was not in class. Some of the other schoolmates who had taken part in the Sportsfest reported that the leaders had, indeed, prolonged the games to the point of exhaustion. The weather had been foul, and the participants were all chilled to the bone. Four days later, Hannelore died of pneumonia. I was stunned, and wept in sorrow as well as frustration.

Frl. Plaas selected Mariane and me to represent the class at the funeral. We had taken up a collection, and selected a funeral wreath which we were to carry to the Diebsteig cemetery via streetcar. We took part in the grave side ceremony. The solemn observance of the placement of the flowers and our class wreath had just been completed, when the broken-hearted parents observed two Hitler Youth leaders step onto the scene. They had arrived late, wanting to present their floral offering decorated with a large red ribbon on which the black swastika on a white field was prominently displayed. The B.D.M. girls deliberately covered our class ribbon with theirs. Hannelore's mother flung the swastika wreath at them with such force and fury, that it left a green stain on the white blouse of one of them.

"Geh' zum Teufel, ihr Lumpen! (Go to the devil, you scoundrels)" she shouted.

Her husband tried to console her, but both were overcome with grief, clutching the casket. Gently, the pastor tried to pull them away. Mariane and I stood crying, and finally managed to find our way back to the streetcar station. At the stop, we saw the two youth leaders. Bitterly, I accused them of murder, and Mariane had to restrain me from striking them.

* * *

My mother had been summoned to the Gestapo in 1938, and my father a year later, for general interrogation. Papa never spoke about it, only to say how thorough they had been in uncovering his original family name. The network of file systems in their bureaucratic world seemed to reach back at least one whole generation, how else would they have determined that we had Americanized our family name? They had demanded that Papa resume the use of his old Lithuanian name, since by their definition that made him very Aryan, and subsequently made us safe. Erika and I, however, were a special case, inasmuch as our names differed from that of our parents', and, being entered upon American birth certificates, could not be tampered with.

America had now entered the war, and my parents and I took advantage of a prisoner of war radio station that broadcast news in English. I found it helpful in keeping up familiarity with my native language, as well as with my school lessons. These broadcasts were sponsored by the German government; to listen to foreign stations could warrant a death penalty.

Herr Becher was late with the rent. That was unusual enough to have caused us some concern, but Papa was earning enough with his overtime to easily meet the mortgage payments, even with the additional burden imposed by the increased amount due to the ten year's tax advance that had been imposed to stake Hitler's military preparations. We were gathered around the radio that evening, listening to the 9:00pm English language German news broadcast. A loud banging on the front door startled us, breaking our concentration. By the time Papa reached the door to the front hall, Herr Becher had entered, followed by several Gestapo men. They pushed my father back into the room. I was stunned, and when I heard the all-too-familiar staccato commands, I began to shake.

"Sofort Mantel anziehen! Los! Sie sind Verhaftet wegen Englisher Sendung!" (Get your coat on immediately! You are under arrest for listening to an English broadcast!")

The same tones I recalled when the Jews and the Gypsies were taken! Now we tried to face down the uniformed men, and stall for time. Mama engaged them in conversation, and explained that what we were listening to was a German broadcast presented in English for the benefit of prisoners of war. They were reluctant to believe my parents, when to our immense relief, the radio announcer made a station identification. I was only dimly aware of a murmured apology by the officer, a touch of the hat, a click of heels, and then the departing roar of a vehicle.

Bombings Increase.

In the autumn of '42, we received an invitation from Tante Auguste and Uncle Ernst to celebrate a "Richtfest" with them and the builders who had just finished the roof framing of their new brick house in Halstenbek. We sent our regrets, but due to our very busy schedule, we explained that we could not come at this time.

"When the house is completed and you move out of Altona, we will make a special trip to inspect the dwelling," Mama wrote in a note to them.

Papa had recovered from his accident, and was on a rigorous schedule at the Howaldt yard, as well as being back to work in his shop. Mama was busy, as usual , with household chores, the management of the apartment house, and scuttling between Rathaus and bank.. We had lived with uncertainty and the fear of death for several years now. It was necessary for us to consciously suppress our anxieties to avoid being devoured by them, often by joking about the regime, imitating Hitler's or Göring's postures, or praying for a speedy end of the war. The bombings continued to increase in frequency and intensity, and we on occasion recklessly watched the aerial battles in the searchlight-illuminated night sky during raids from the dubious security of our bedroom window. Our earliest shelter consisted of the makeshift precautions my father had set up in our own cellar, but when the bunker at the Schaumburg Strasse, near Johannisstrasse was completed, Mama, Erika, and I took cover there. We would fearfully hurry, carrying our carefully selected survival luggage with us at the first strains of the air raid sirens. Papa always stayed at home, although I never understood how he could sleep through the raids. He felt that his long hours of work and production quotas made it essential for him to get as much rest as conditions would permit.

Bombings notwithstanding, life had to go on as usual. I attended school, church, violin lessons, practiced with Elfriede, exercised in the Museum gym, and visited the Altona Museum with friends. I also still managed to take in movies with Irmgard, enjoying our favorite UFA stars Theo Lingen, Maritta Röck, Zahra Leander, or Heinz Rühmann.

Günther was at Irmgard's house one day when we came home from seeing "Quax der Bruchpilot," our favorite comedy. We felt a special tension when we found him in the black uniform of the Panzer Division. Gentle touches of hands, and light jesting masked our unexpressed emotions.

"Hals und Beinbruch!" I joked, not wishing to reveal my true feelings.

"Unkraut vergeht nicht!" Irmgard snapped.

When I shook hands with Günther as he left, I had a premonition that we would never see him alive again.

That night we were privileged not to have our sleep interrupted by air raids, but I was awakened by the popping of corks, and what I took to be the sound of gushing champagne. Mama heard me get up, and called me to come to their bedroom. They had turned on the night stand light, and were laughing hysterically. The black currant juice in bottles which were stored on top of their chifforobe had fermented, exploded the stoppers, and sprayed the dark juice and pulpy ink- colored mash all over the pale yellow-flowered wallpaper, the ceiling, bed sheets, and my parent's faces and hair. We laughed until our sides hurt, and then spent the rest of the night cleaning up the mess.

* * *

My violin found itself tucked under my chin every day, and when the rowdy teenage boys on the street heard me practice, they would shout, "Paganini!" At first, I was much annoyed at being taunted, but when I came face to face with some of the ruffians, they would turn out to be very polite, and even offer to carry my instrument or my sheet music filled briefcase.

When Irmgard and I met, our conversations would now mostly be about boys, and we vowed to tell each other whoever had "die erste Liebeserklärung" (first declaration of love), or the first kiss. Anything further was not under consideration, for we were ardent romantics, and sex had not yet entered our vocabularies. We did, however, know about the large red light district off the Reeperbahn. The street entrances were obscured by barriers, and were usually spoken of in whispers, which aroused our curiosity. I would pass by some of them on my walk to Herr Pahl's studio, and crane my neck to read what was written on the outside walls, but never really dared to go up close enough.

Irmgard had become very suspicious of her grandmother's occupation.

"She has most peculiar working hours," my friend remarked, "and at times, heavily perfumed and painted women stay at her house. My grandmother forbids me to go near or even to speak to them."

This was most intriguing indeed, and we decided to play detective, and follow her grandmother at the next opportunity.

Our time was carefully accounted for, except on Saturdays, when I could stretch out my schedule with Elfriede, or perhaps when I had errands to do. The opportunity arose because of Herr Pahl's huge tomcat. It was difficult enough to secure the food required by humans; dogs and cats could only be kept by people who had certain advantages in food supplies, or the time to stand in line at a special store which dealt exclusively in entrails. Animals were guarded for fear of being abducted; rumor had it that they would wind up as sausages. Herr Pahl cherished and protected his cat, and coerced his students to stand in line for him at the entrails store, delivering the bounty to Frau Pahl. One afternoon, when it was my turn to do the shopping for the cat's food, Irmgard and I decided that we would follow her grandmother when she left for work later on. Irmgard was waiting for me in front of the Karzentra store on the Grosse Bergstrasse. I was carrying the package of entrails for the cat. We spotted her grandmother heading towards the Nobistor, turning the corner of the Grosse Freiheit, and disappearing into one of the side streets that looked as though it were closed by a gate, but in reality were staggered partitions. Timidly, we darted into the great beyond, and spotted the house where the door was just closing. The moment we entered the forbidden street, we were observed. Windows were noisily

115

opened, and shrill female voices shouted obscenities. The contents of a chamber pot was poured down from a second floor window, narrowly missing us, and I dropped the package for Herr Pahl's cat. A redheaded woman in a green gown picked it up and refused to give up her find. A black haired, lace-robed madame with long, lacquered fingernails threatened me with a broom, and we bolted out of the red light zone. Panting, I arrived at Herr Pahl's studio while Irmgard waited in the hall.

"I dropped the package for the cat, and a strange woman picked it up," were my mournful words to Frau Pahl, as I explained the circumstances.

"That breed is getting bolder and bolder," she chuckled. "What a surprise she's going to have when she opens the package!"

I promised to stand in line again for the feline ration, and so the cat was promised yet another meal.

The following Sunday I once again met Irmgard at the movies. We enjoyed "der Muster Gatte," another hilariously funny Heinz Rühmann film, but "the ideal husband" was far from our minds. Irmgard had asked her grandmother about her trip behind the forbidden partition, and had been informed that she was a health inspector for the red light district. The city's most notorious quarter is ironically named after a saint, St. Pauli. The neighborhood has hundreds of rowdy and intimate bars, strip joints, a wax museum, theaters, operetta house, and oddly enough, my favorite, the Ernst Drucker Platt-Deutsche Bühne. This Elizabethan style theater features performances in the low-German dialect.

* * *

The ubiquitous uniforms of the military and the S.A. were visible only to small degree on our block. Herr Becher wore his party attire on Sundays and special occasions, such as the May 1st celebration, the Bismarck event, and what was called "Sammeln für Winterhilfswerk." The latter was a nationwide welfare fund drive. Schools were closed, and every household had to pledge financial support or volunteer involvement.

On one such a collection day, a traumatic incident occurred. I did not have to attend school, and Herr Becher delivered a red tin can to us to be used for collections. We were, of course, leery of his behavior, especially after the radio broadcast incident. He had attempted to alleviate his frustration at not having been able to have us arrested by such petty tactics as being late with the rent. When my father had gone up to collect, an altercation had ensued in which Herr Becher had tried to push Papa down the stairs. He was rewarded for his efforts with a fist in his eye. He had good reason to hide his face for several days after this incident. The black eye was not exactly a swastika badge to be shown off to the neighbors. We accepted the collection can from him, thinking it expedient not to make further waves over the fracas. As middle class landlords, we felt that it was incumbent upon us to participate in the fund drive. I in fact looked forward to spending a day as a gregarious salesgirl. Beautifully crafted souvenir pendants were the items to be sold, and I visited the designated pickup station to obtain my quota of articles. I was given a box full of ribbon-strung transparent disks in various colors, engraved with the likenesses of great composers, such as Bach, Brahms, Beethoven, and Schubert. I encountered many of my school chums plying their items on the Grosse and Kleine Bergstrasse, Blücherstrasse, and my own neighborhood, so I decided to try my luck in less frequented areas. What came to mind as a certain sale, was my music teacher, Herr Pahl. He would practically swoon at the mere mention of the "3 B's." I was sure that I could probably sell him a good part of my supplies, and then spend the rest of the day in the Hamburg museum, or walk to the Speckstrasse to visit the house Brahms had lived in. Herr and Frau Pahl did indeed buy a complete series each, and the remainder were sold at various business establishments displaying the little metal plaque with the motto "Der Deutsche Gruss ist Heil Hitler" (the German greeting is Heil Hitler).

Before noon, my red cannister was heavy with coins, and the cardboard display box being empty, I was making my way back to the pickup station to return the proceeds. As I hurried along the Holstenwall, a military truck passed by me. It screeched to a stop a short distance ahead, and several S.S. men leaped off in a clatter of boots. Visions of the abduction of my Gypsy friends flashed through my mind, and, for reasons obscure to me to this day, I approached them, and accused them of this deed. Perhaps it was the sight of the uniforms, the clicking of the metal shod heels, or the recognition of voice patterns. I was in a fury, and when they surrounded me, I lashed out at them with my metal cannister. They attempted to force me into a building, away from prying eyes. The officer I had managed to strike gave me a hard push, and I fell against the stone corner of the entrance. A sharp pain took my breath away, and I doubled over, still clutching the tin can. I recovered enough presence of mind to wave the can about, and loudly proclaim that it had to be delivered to the Führer's welfare fund. That statement was my salvation. The men hurriedly vanished into the building, and I somehow made my way across the street to the park-like area outside the Hamburg museum. It took me several hours of rest on a bench to recover from the ordeal sufficiently to be able to get back on my way home. Late that afternoon, I hobbled to the streetcar stop, and rode to the Grosse Bergstrasse. I could barely walk when I reached the Bürgerstrasse, when to my relief, a classmate I met on the way invited me into her mother's hat shop to rest. I did not tell them how I came to be injured, nor did I tell my parents until years later.

Hamburg is Destroyed.

In July of 1943, we planned a picnic with Elfriede and her family. Mama had even persuaded Papa to come along. She brushed off his American made mauve tweed knicker suit that he had gotten from Averil Harriman, and Erika and I wore frocks made by Mama's dressmaker. We looked forward to the electric train ride to Poppenbüttel, eyeing the basket of goodies we were taking to the outing to be shared with our friends and their grandparents with eager anticipation.

That night, the alarm sirens howled again. I carefully placed my pretty pink outfit over the chair next to my bed, put on my school dress to go to the air raid shelter, grabbed my violin case with one hand, and the briefcase with documents and a change of underwear with the other. I had performed this routine dozens of times, and we were quite efficient at speedily gathering in the hall. Mama, Erika , and I rushed out into the dark like seasoned night stalkers. We joined neighbors, among them my schoolmate Marga and her mother. We dashed into the Schaumburg Strasse, our progress gradually being impeded by the throngs of people surrounding us. All carried at least one piece of luggage, held a blanket, or clutched an infant. Everyone appeared to perform these nightly excursions in zombie-like trances. We were intimately familiar with every curb or crack in the sidewalks. The outside wall of the yet unfinished bunker still had the scaffolding attached, as the camouflage scheme and the steel portholes had thus far not been applied or installed.

119

"Watch your steps!" the air raid warden cautioned the shelter-seekers. "Our illustrious mayor has sent his own family out to the Lüneburger Heide for the duration." I was always impressed at the good natured jesting that people were able to engage in even under such conditions of duress.

We filed into the shelter. The lower level was already completely occupied by clusters of families and individuals, so we were directed to the next level, one flight up. Although the bunker provided several stories, the lower ones were preferred, for obvious reasons. The bombs had become more and more powerful, capable of penetrating yards of steel mesh-reinforced concrete like butter. We settled onto a long wooden bench, squeezed together like chickens in a roosting coop.

As we huddled in nervous anticipation, an ominous rumbling grew in volume, accompanied by sharp vibrations. The menacing drone of what sounded like many hundreds of aircraft engines filled the air, interrupted by the jarring vibrations of exploding bombs. Clouds of dust poured in through the unfinished portholes and doors, yet noone panicked, and few even cried out. Mama, Erika, and I formed a cloverleaf, clinging to each other with our blanket over our heads. It soon became unbearably hot, as the outside scaffolding was burning, and smoke was permeating the entire building. The warden advised everyone to lie on the floor to minimize the effects of the smoke. The lights began to flicker, and soon went out, leaving us in complete darkness. The moaning of a woman near us was heard. Someone turned on a flashlight, and we found that a baby had been born a few feet away from us. We could provide but little comfort to the poor, hysterical woman after the infant died. Even with several flashlights attempting to illuminate the room, it was difficult to see through the thick smoke.

My nostrils were filled with soot, and my dry lips got no relief from a sandpaper tongue. The handkerchief I was clutching soon became grimy with my own sweat. I needed water desperately, but the little that remained in the uncompleted supply area was being used for aid to those burn victims or wounded who had failed to reach the shelter after the mass attack had begun. It was a raging inferno outside, and inside, we felt that we would expire from the smoke that choked our mouths and throats. I desperately tried to clear my nostrils and ears with my perspiration soaked hankie. Just as I was about to pass out from thirst, a man who had braved the walls of fire came back with two half-filled pails of murky water.

Each person in our immediate area was permitted to dip the corner of a handkerchief into the lukewarm liquid. I sucked on the moisturized cloth as if it were a pacifier, and fell into an exhausted slumber.

Eerie, poisonous looking green and yellow rays of light streamed through the portholes and now wide open doors. I realized it was morning. Mama felt me stirring; we were still tightly clutched together. We were alive! Erika was still sleeping, and we tried not to awaken her. I knew what Mama was thinking. I saw how she craned her neck when a shadow crossed the door opening. We looked for a male silhouette, hoping it would be my father. The warden and several neighbors gave us brief snatches of reports. Marga's father had been on leave from the Russian front, and had lamented that it seemed to be more dangerous here at home. He, too, stayed in his apartment when the sirens had announced the raid, but when he had heard the tremendous drone of the first waves of attacking planes, he had dashed to shelter. On passing our house, he had seen my father carrying buckets of sand from our backyard, and chopping away debris from the adjacent house. That summer, Hamburg received a systematic incendiary carpet bombing. These bombs spread flames over large areas upon ignition, augmenting the destruction of the ordinary explosive devices. The U.S. Air Force dropped more than 1,500,000 tons of bombs on Germany in WWII. 300,000 homes and historical buildings were destroyed in Hamburg during the July raids alone.

Papa was a lonely fire fighter, trying to smother an inferno with shovelfuls of sand, and a trickling hose. We knew that he was out there somewhere, but had he survived the tremendous heat and the fires which had been generated by the windstorms driving the all-devouring flames? The asphalted streets had melted from the heat, trapping hapless fleeing victims, and incinerating them. As we stood outside the door of the bunker, we surveyed the destruction surrounding us. The bunker was the only structure remaining standing amidst a panorama of crumpled bricks and smoldering heaps of rubble. We realized that it would be senseless to head towards the Lahrmannstrasse. No semblance of order remained; our street no longer existed. All the houses in the entire area had simply vanished. We were engulfed in a haze of smoke, gazing into the gates of hell. The sun hung unreally, like a chartreuse illuminated ball behind a veil of burning vapor. We hopped like frightened rabbits across the Grosse Bergstrasse, looking for a path to safely place our singed soles. One thought occupied our minds- water, water.

The warden had mentioned a possible gathering place of bombed-out victims at the cold storage facility. I was familiar with this structure, which stood down by the Elbe. The goal of reaching the river spurred us on. Skirting burnt bodies, leaping over unexploded bombs, three bewildered zombies made their way to the river. The world around us seemed unreal, just a nightmare from which we would soon awaken. The smell of roasted human flesh mingling with the odors from the smoldering butcher shop drove home the terrible reality of the death and destruction everywhere around us.

We could see the water now, and sections of the sidewalk and street were still intact. Clusters of people perching on suitcases and bags lined the river's edge. The siren on the roof of the cold storage building wailed a warning of another attack, and I hurried to at least dip my arms into the cooling water. My mother urgently tugged me away, and we hustled into awesome darkness of the building's cellar. A few temporary lights seemed to accentuate the low temperature, and created a mortuary-like atmosphere. Now I became chilly with the thought of being entombed, and began shivering uncontrollably. The Elbe had been covered in rainbow-colored oil slicks, and my arms now felt slimy to the touch. Mama was speaking with Marga's mother, whom we chanced to meet in the cellar. Marga, Erika, and I squatted in a corner, leaning against one another, listening to our mothers' conversation.

Mama asked the same anxious question, "Have you seen my husband?"

"Not since my husband saw him at the beginning of the raid. He was trying to put out the flames."

We sat staring into empty space, only half aware of our surroundings until the all-clear sounded, and then emerged like moles, squinting at the unreal, jaundiced sunball. The Red Cross arrived, scurrying about like so many erratic white ants, with the emblem of their organization visible on hats or armbands. I breathed a sigh of hope, whispering- "Water!" to the nurse. She handed me a steaming hot cup of thick barley soup, our first nutriment in 16 hours. I gagged on the fatty pieces of bacon, but skimmed the sparse liquid greedily.

A loudspeaker mounted on a passing vehicle barked out all but unintelligible instructions to bombed-out victims, directing them to assemble at the Neumühlen dock, where they would be ferried to Blankenese. Automatically, we stood up, grasped the baggage that comprised the only material goods we had left in the world, and shuffled along with the throngs of bombed-out refugees.

The vessel filled with humanity quickly. The usually picturesque trip began with apprehension and gloom. All of us were grimy and sooty. We looked forward eagerly to the promised water and cold drinks upon arrival at the Ferry Restaurant. We immediately collapsed onto a bench as the ship chugged north to Blankenese. Upon arrival, we slowly walked across the gangplank while deeply inhaling the relatively cleaner, smoke-free air. We stood in line to take turns washing up in the tiny ladies' room of the "Fährehaus," guzzling large swallows of water from our cupped hands. Although we managed to remove some of the dirt and grime covering us, we still carried the odors of a charred smokehouse. We arranged ourselves as comfortably as possible in the main dining room. The hall had been normally closed due to the prohibition of dancing, but all available space was now crammed with the homeless. Local women brought powdered artificial fruit drinks. The proprietor watched the sorry lot of non-paying customers gloomily as large batches of the drinks were mixed. We sat forlorn, seemingly ignored, when a kindly middle-aged woman approached Mama. She introduced herself as "Frau Henze," and asked if we would like to stay with her and her daughter. She had realized that everyone in Blankenese would probably be required to take in refugees, and had taken the initiative to look for people she would feel comfortable with. She helped carry our belongings as we followed her to the door. An official stood next to the restaurant owner, carefully listing our names along with that of Frau Henze. As we scrambled after her, we became aware that she was quite accustomed to climbing the steep hillside of this quaint coastal community. She led us to a cozy, neat cottage. A teenaged girl who was waiting for us had already prepared two single beds in a charming attic room. Water was being heated on a gas stove, and a portable wash stand was placed in the room for our use. Exhausted, without adequate sleep for the last thirty hours, we sank into oblivion, waking late the following day.

After enjoying the breakfast Frau Henze had prepared for us, Mama decided to take the ferry into Hamburg. The two women had already started strong bonds of friendship, as often occurs in times of great stress. Frau Henze had recently become a widow. Her husband had been a submarine commander, and had been lost at the Skaggerack sea battle. We admired the handsome portrait of the uniformed officer gracing her bedroom dresser, and shed tears for him as well as for my father.

Erika, Frau Henze's daughter Helga, and I walked Mama to the ferry. When the ferry departed, we lolled at the beach for a while, then meandered back up the winding hillside street. Blankenese had been one of my favorite Sunday excursion objectives. We had taken the ferry trip upon several occasions to enjoy this unpretentious fishing village. Now it had become our temporary haven, after surviving a hellish inferno. We anxiously awaited Mama's return. She arrived alone, crestfallen and discouraged. The following day, she sallied forth into the city once more. This time, she had good news upon her return. Papa had been seen after the raid.

"He's alive!" Neighbors had confirmed it, and knew that he was hospitalized, but did not know where.

The Blankenese warden issued special ration cards to the refugees. Mama took us shopping in a small local department store, where we were some of the fortunate ones to acquire a change of clothes.

The next day, she traveled to Altona again, placing a note with our new address in a bottle upon a small pyramid she built on the smoldering pile of rubble that had been our home.

That evening, the terrifying droning of aircraft engines awakened us. Mama, Erika , and I leaped to the window, watched the bombers pass overhead, and wondered if their targets would once again be Hamburg, or if our relatives in Kiel would be the recipients.

In the morning, the warden came by to tell us that we would only be permitted to stay in Blankenese for another two days. All the homeless in our group were to report to the police station. We were to be bumped inland in order to make room for the victims of the last raid. Mama immediately left for Altona in a last desperate effort to locate my father before being re-located.

Erika and I waited with apprehension at the ferry pier that evening. As the ferry eased up to the dock, a crewman signaled his intent to cast the docking lines; like an old salt, I caught the hawser and threw a clove hitch over a bollard, the way I had seen the maneuver performed dozens of times at the Landungsbrücken wharf. Then we saw Papa standing next to my mother, a black patch covering his one good eye.

Erika muttered, "What happened to Papa?"

Both of them were carrying luggage, but Papa's step was slow and unsure. Mama was carefully guiding him. I realized that he was not able to see at all, since the patch was covering his only good eye, the other one being artificial.

"He's blind!" I whispered to Erika as I helped him lift his suitcase to the bench. I felt his hand gently touch the top of my head. My mother took a small flask and some cotton balls out of her handbag. She removed the patch from my father's eye, exposing a drenched piece of gauze, and carefully wiped his infected eyelid. Then she tilted his head back, and squeezed three drops of liquid into the eye.

"In another day or so, your father will be able to see again," she informed us, reassuring Papa at the same time. We were told that the intense flare of incendiary bombs had caused his temporary blindness.

Slowly, we climbed up the terraced bank of the Elbe. Neither of my parents were aware of the unexpected beauty of the constantly changing vistas at every turn of the road. The river and the evening sun were putting on a spectacular display of diffused, contrasting rays of light. I hurried on ahead while my parents and Erika struggled laboriously along the cobblestone path. After depositing the suitcase I was carrying, I dashed back to help them with the rest of their bundles. Stopping for a brief moment to drink in the tranquil scene, I folded my hands in prayer, thanking God for his protection. To be certain that my prayer would not be missed, I repeated it in English , as well.

Frau Henze and her daughter rejoiced with us, and we gathered in their living room for a small celebration. Papa had removed the eye patch, and Mama had been carefully washing and medicating the area per the doctor's instructions. Our gnawing hunger was stilled by portions of fried potatoes washed down with mugfulls of ersatz coffee. We raised our cups to toast Papa's survival, and wished each other continued good luck.

"I was playing at sleeping," my father recounted, "pretending not to hear the droning of the aircraft engines after the sirens had stopped howling, But I became too restless to stay in bed." So began his narrative. He had put on his work clothes, since it was simply not in his nature to be idle, even under such circumstances.

He went down to his workshop, carefully pulled down the shades, and drew closed the heavy drapes to ensure that no light would emanate from the windows. Activating his wood-turning lathe, he continued his manufacture of small handcart wheel spokes. The noise of the machine drowned out much of the noise of the attack, but then the lights began to flicker, and the power abruptly ceased. Grasping his flashlight, he went outside to ascertain the situation. The backyard and the adjoining garden were glaring as bright as daylight, incendiary bombs spewing intense phosphorescence.

He beat out the fire burning along the fence with water-soaked blankets, and tried to remove anything flammable from contact with the house. Our building was constructed of heavy stone, and he hoped to be able to save it from the flames. As he looked up, he saw the sky raining assorted shapes and sizes of incendiary devices, which exploded upon contact with the ground, spewing molten combustion everywhere. He retreated to the cellar and attempted to stem the spread of the flames with sand and his short garden hose, which had been connected to the kitchen sink. An ear-blasting clap, like the loudest thunderbolt shook the ground under him. There had been a direct hit to the neighboring house. Muffled cries of help could be heard through the brick partition separating the next door cellar from ours. Papa smashed through the barrier with a sledge hammer, thankful that he had previously taken the precaution to open an aperture in the one meter thick stone cellar wall separating the adjacent buildings. He helped the retired couple and their grandchild to escape from their rubble filled basement, while thick smoke and clouds of dust poured through the opening. Water was gushing from burst pipes; fallen plaster and a veritable confetti of glass shards covered all. A few moments later, the remainder of the neighbor's house collapsed, the lucky residents saved from certain death only in the nick of time.

After the rescue, the couple and the girl recovered their composure in our basement, while Papa continued unsuccessfully with his efforts to save our house from the ravages of fire. In the distance, the wailing of fire trucks could be heard, all but drowned out by the din of collapsing wood and stone structures and the crashing of glass. He realized that his fight with the inferno was futile. Hurriedly, he threw some of our coats and dresses into suitcases, and stuffed in our New York family photo album between some of my violin sheet music.

The top floors of our apartment house were already in bright yellow flames, smoke was pouring through the broken windows, which had burst from the heat and shrapnel impacts. It was high time to abandon the building. He collected the baggage, and urged his three charges to follow him out into the cobblestone street. They darted along the Dennerstrasse to take refuge at the fruit and vegetable store in the Bürgerstrasse. Papa once more returned to our burning house to retrieve any further household articles he could salvage, bundled them in bedspreads, and stored them in the back room of the green grocer. Tempting fate, he went back again, this time to rescue some of his hand tools. The destruction of his workshop distressed him most of all of our losses. He was choking from the smoke, could barely see out of his only eye, which was tearing profusely, and barely made it back to the relative safety of the store. The owner promised to safeguard our valuables for us.

Looting began almost immediately, despite the threat of the death penalty if caught in the act. Undeterred by this warning, several looters were captured and executed on the spot.

* * *

We who had been rooting for a quick Allied victory, luckily survived the vast destruction that they had rained on Hamburg, the city I had learned to love. I thought of the magnificent churches, the theaters, concert halls, opera house, and puppetry whose performances I had enjoyed, and my many visits to the Hamburg museum. Now the horizon surrounding the metropolis was covered by a gigantic pall of smoke. I surveyed the deadly, curling, snake-like vapors from the vantage point of the peak of the Süllberg in Blankenese, recalling the nauseous odors of the burning corpses trapped in the molten street asphalt.

Had Elfriede and her parents survived? What about my school teachers? My music teacher, Herr Pahl, who had been a student of Humperdinck, suffered from angina. Could he withstand the anxiety brought on by the horrors of the stupendous bombing, which were almost too much for even a young, healthy person like myself to endure? He and Frau Pahl were fragile senior citizens, so were Elfriede's grandparents. Would I ever find them again, if they, too, had been bombed out of their home? I realized that it had become necessary to totally destroy the Hitler regime, with its fanatical "today Germany, tomorrow the whole world" objective, but the dubious necessity of obliterating entire cities, with their age-old cultural heritages, simply eluded me. I feared that along with these losses, I might after all never get to see the imposing skyscrapers of Manhattan again. Would all off my familiar architectural friends be lost to me forever? We had survived this initial holocaust, but there was no way of knowing how much more we would have to endure before the madness came to an end. Will I ever see America again?

Helen and Parents

Tante Grete and Helen

Papa in Texas

Uncle Hans with Helen

Post card of the S.S. Roosevelt

Helen at Shuffleboard

Post card of Times Square
at night

Gemeindeverwaltung der Hansestadt Hamburg
Schulverwaltung

Volksschule *für Mädchen Lürienstr. 3*

Halbjahreszeugnis

für *Helen Howaldt*

geboren den *31. Januar* 1930

Klasse: *2b*   Schuljahr 19*38/39*

Helen's first German report card

The Howaldt group at the Baltic Sea health camp in Haffkrug

Reichsmusikkammer Fachschaft Musikerzieher

Unterrichtsbedingungen

Erfüllungsort: Hamburg.

Zwischen Herrn Hartwig Pahl, Hamburg, Koopertahn 27/29 als Lehrer

und Herrn Blyszus, Hamburg-Altona, Lehrmannstr.16. als Schüler

bzw.

als gesetzlichem Vertreter des Schülers ist heute folgende Vereinbarung getroffen worden:

1. Der unterzeichnete Lehrer übernimmt den Unterricht der Tochter Helen

(Name des Schülers) in (Fach) Violine

Contract with music teacher, Herr Pahl, exempting Helen form Hitler Youth Activities

Die Impfanstalt in Hamburg.   **Impfbezirk Hamburg.**

Impfschein

über eine der gesetzlichen Pflicht genügende Pockenschutz-Wiederimpfung.

Impfliste Nr. 2591 IV   Hamburg, den 22. September 1942

Helen Blesens

geboren 31. Januar 1930, wurde am 15. September 1942 zum **ersten Male** mit Erfolg gegen Pocken wiedergeimpft.

Durch diese Impfung ist die gesetzliche Pflicht (gemäß Impfgesetz vom 8. April 1874) genügt.

Dr. W. Lehmann.

Vordr. 384a/V. J. 84 des Polizeipräsidenten in Hamburg.

Vaccination Certificate   Helen at 13 years of age

Order Form

To order additional copies, fill out this form and send it along with your check or money order to: American Hamburger
                             Helen Buchholtz
                             79 Clubhouse Dr.
                             Palm Coast, FL 32137.

Cost per copy $11.95 plus $2.50 P&H.

Ship _____ copies of *American Hamburger* to:

Name_____

Address:_____

Address:_____

Address:_____

❏   **Check box for signed copy**

DATE DUE